Earth's Darkness and Light:

Understanding the World We Live In

Servants of the Living God

Boyd Aaron George

And

Dr Pamela Atieno Odhiambo Abuodha

Contents

Copyright

Copyright © March 2014 by Boyd A. George & Pamela A.O. Abuodha

Unless otherwise indicated, Scripture is taken from the New King James Version. Copyright © 1982 by Thomas Nelson, Inc. Used by permission. All rights reserved.

Scripture marked ESV is taken from The Holy Bible, English Standard Version, copyright © 2001 by Crossway Bibles, a division of Good News Publishers. Used by permission. All rights reserved.

Note: All uses of the first person "I" refer to Boyd George.

Edited by Christian Editing Services, USA.

Interior and cover designs by the authors.

Printed by CreateSpace, An Amazon.com Company.

Available from Amazon estore or Smashwords estore.

Emails: tamisotlgbooks@yahoo.com or bagnpam@yahoo.com

Website: www.tamii.org created and maintained by the authors.

ISBN: ISBN-13: 978-0-9923279-2-7

TWELVE APOSTLE MINISTRIES INTERNATIONAL INC.

And I, if I am lifted up from the earth, will draw all *peoples* to Myself.
John 12:32

Dedication

This book is dedicated to all those who read it and allow the Spirit of the Lord to guide them, change them, and make for them a better life here on earth and in eternity with God.

Table of Contents

	Acknowledgments	vi
	Introduction	1
1	**How It All Began**	**5**
1.1	Battle in Heaven	8
1.2	Existing Powers over the Earth	36
1.3	The Earth's Creation and Man's Dominion	43
1.4	Prayer Guide for Chapter 1	50
2	**The Genesis of Kingdoms and Nations**	**53**
2.1	The Fall of Mankind	72
2.2	God's Reaction and Provision	84
2.3	Life Outside of Eden	96
2.4	Prayer Guide for Chapter 2	104
3	**Not All That Glitters Is Gold**	**107**
3.1	Mankind Deceived	109
3.2	Deception—A Way of Life Today	131
3.3	The Power of Good Versus Evil	145
3.4	Prayer Guide for Chapter 3	152
4	**Does Life after Death Actually Exist?**	**157**
4.1	Why Did Adam Hide from God?	171
4.2	Accountability a Way of Life	180
4.3	Accountability Demanded by God	190
4.4	Prayer Guide for Chapter 4	201

5	**Darkness and Light on the Earth**	**205**
5.1	Darkness over and in Mankind	213
5.2	Light over and in Mankind	221
5.3	Personal Evaluation	233
5.4	Prayer Guide for Chapter 5	248
	Notes	253

Acknowledgements

> And I thank Christ Jesus our Lord who has enabled me, because He counted me faithful, putting me into the ministry, although I was formerly a blasphemer, a persecutor, and an insolent man; but I obtained mercy because I did it ignorantly in unbelief. (1 Timothy 1:12–13)

We are most grateful to God through our Lord and Savior Jesus Christ for finding us and choosing us for His service and for using us as channels to download His thoughts and mind to the churches and nations. Our role has simply been to write it all down. To God be the glory, as our joy becomes full. We acknowledge that it is only by God's grace we have written this book and that God is rightfully the author.

We also are thankful for the works of others that we have referenced to make our message clear. Such works include dictionaries, Bible commentaries, and research on various subjects.

Upcoming books by these authors:

Heaven Full of Surprises: Deception of Grace Today in the Church

The Timeline of the Church: Preparation of the Church for the Time of the Rapture

Contents

Introduction

> The thief does not come except to steal, and to kill, and to destroy. I have come that they may have life, and that they may have it more abundantly. (John 10:10)

Earth's Darkness and Light highlights the tensions and calamities mankind faces in the world today and reveals four different orders that are responsible for what is happening on the earth. *Earth's Darkness and Light* is a thoughtful and conversational book that helps you ask questions you may never have thought of asking before. It helps you look at the pros and cons of life and encourages you to decide to live life better, rather than give in to despair and not even try to live.

This book deals with practical issues and asks thoughtful questions to help you think through these issues and make decisions that will allow you to experience a life accompanied by the five pillars of life. These five pillars of life are love, peace, joy, contentment, and freedom—the things all people earnestly yearn for but seldom know where to look. This book will prompt you to ask yourselves important questions and to define what life really is to you.

You may be a billionaire or have a good job that pays well, but if you still lack contentment, is that life? You may be among the working class, working hard and trying to make ends meet. You may not even have a job and depend on government welfare to sustain you (or you may live in a country with no government welfare). But if you lack peace, do you consider that life? If we do not wake up from our slumber, we will leave this world without even trying to live and experience true life. If others can experience it, however, you and I can do the same. We can enjoy a life enriched with the five pillars.

Earth's Darkness and Light reveals the sad results of mankind's inability to foresee and grasp the true peace and freedom everyone needs. Instead of freedom, we have been put under the bondage of deception, which glitters like gold but offers nothing of value. The more we accept this fool's gold, which we like to think will solve our problems and set us free, the more tightly we find ourselves bound. This deception has become a way of life in our time. We need to wake up to the truth that while this fool's gold looks real, it is not real at all. It leads us only into a vain attempt to "catch the wind."

Earth's Darkness and Light describes man's origin and the drift away from His creator God, a drift that has caused him immeasurable harm. This book also speaks of the need to return to our Creator, and the *only* way back is through our Lord and Savior Jesus Christ. It reveals the power within mankind that we call the fourth order. This is the order of the *power* to choose *(willpower)*. This fourth order manifests the third order and brings into existence the first and second orders. The first order is the *order of darkness*. The second order is the *order of light*. The third order is the *order of dos and don'ts*. *Earth's Darkness and Light* is designed to help us realize the world of fantasy in which we live and to bring us into reality so we can choose light over darkness.

Earth's Darkness and Light talks of the greater orders that operate over and within mankind. It also addresses crucial questions: If there is a God, why am I being hurt? If there is a God, why did my family die and leave me? If there is a God, why is there so much evil in the world? The questions are endless, but this book seeks to honestly answer, or enable the reader to answer, most of the important questions we can ask. You will discover as you read *Earth's Darkness and Light* how much influence you have because you have the power to choose and make this life of yours a better life. "Arise; shine; for your light has come! And the glory of the Lord is risen upon you" (Isaiah 60:1).

Introduction

Chapter One

How It All Began

"My people are destroyed for lack of knowledge" (Hosea 4:6), the prophet wrote. While I have been a Christian for many years, it was not until recently that by the grace of God I had the opportunity to receive some wonderful insights from God's Word. In my youth as a Christian, I did not understand what the church was all about. However, I experienced great love and joy whenever I was in God's presence. There could have been people in the church I didn't like, but that all changed whenever we were in the presence of the Lord.

As a young man growing up with my mates, I remember some of the awkward—and wayward—moments of my life, such as coveting, gambling, and even immorality. Nevertheless, I always loved the church. I got involved in the church in my childhood days; as I grew up; I became a part of the music department of our church and was involved in other activities in and around the church as well. I remember one day after a prayer meeting being outside with my mates and thoroughly enjoying the moment. I looked up to heaven without understanding what I was saying or doing at the time, and I spoke to God. "Oh God, may I praise you until people can be healed and set free from their bondages."

In 1990 I experienced war in my country of Liberia for the first time in my life. It kept me close to the church but not close to God. When the war subsided, I joined a secular band, and we began to play from one disco club or disco pub to another. At the same time, I was going to church on Sundays to play the organ for the services. It didn't take long for me to realize I was having mixed emotions about playing in the pubs while also playing in the church. Jesus said, "No one can serve two masters; for either he will hate the one and love the other, or else he will be loyal to the one and despise the other. You cannot serve God and mammon" (Matthew 6:24). As the Bible says, one desire begins to dominate the other. Initially, when I found myself playing in the pubs and at church at the same time, I thought it was cool. However, I soon began to realize that playing in the pub was not as enjoyable as playing in the church. In fact, I started hating playing in the pub, but I did not stop.

     Sometimes we find ourselves doing something we hate but we continue doing it anyway. This could be because it's our source of income or because of fear of what would happen if we left the job. I was in that situation. Playing in the pubs was a source of income for me. But by the grace of God, He drew me to Himself. Jesus said, "No one can come to Me unless the Father who sent Me draws him" (John 6:44).

     I pretended all was well on the outside, but the contradictory and mixed emotions I was experiencing made me restless on the inside. There was a war going on in my body. At this time, the music department of the church decided to go through a time of separation to the

Lord through fasting and prayer. I can remember as if it were today! I came from band practice and said to myself, "Let me see what is happening at the church," without knowing the Spirit of God was drawing me and working on my behalf. The psalmist said, "Come and see the works of God; He is awesome in His doing toward the sons of men" (Psalm 66:5).

It was around 3:00 p.m., and I went and sat among the brethren without preparing myself through prayer. We began to sing and praise the Lord, which I enjoyed doing. In no time, because of the presence of the Lord in that place, I found myself repenting and saying words that have changed my life. "God, if You have a purpose for my life, let me know Your Word." I did not know what I was saying neither did I plan this prayer. Yet, to my surprise God heard that prayer.

You may or may not identify with this experience, but this kind of thing still happens today. If we allow ourselves to be pulled in the direction that brings us joy and honor among our family, friends, and community, I can tell you it will be well with us. Jesus said, "He who believes in Me, as the Scripture has said, out of his heart will flow rivers of living water" (John 7:38). I could not believe how quick it was and what a blessing it was when God opened the door for me to learn His Word. I quit playing in the pubs and set my heart on God, who had a plan for my life. I did not know what that plan was, but I trusted that God's plan for my life was better than the one I had for myself. Indeed, as God said in His Word, "I know the thoughts that I think toward you, says the LORD, thoughts of peace and not of evil, to give you a future and a hope" (Jeremiah 29:11). Truly, God is the source of our life.

In 1991, I entered the Monrovia Bible Training Centre, where I began to know God and not just learn about Him. My desire for God escalated above everything the world could offer me. I heard God speaking to me through His Word, and as His word came to me; my desire to fulfill it grew and continued to grow even until now. It is my desire to know, understand, reveal, and interpret the Word of God in our time. Today, knowledge has increased in our world, just as the Bible foretold in Daniel 12:4. This increased knowledge, however, causes God's Word to be watered down and misinterpreted at times.

1.1   Battle in Heaven

Let us first define the terms *battle* and *conflict*. The Oxford Dictionaries define *battle* as "a sustained fight between large, organized armed forces." It can also be defined as a fight or "struggle tenaciously to achieve or resist something."[1] On the other hand, the Free Dictionary by Farlex defines *conflict* as "a state of open, often prolonged fighting; a battle or war or a state of disharmony between incompatible persons, ideas, interests; a clash."[2]

Thus, a battle is often part of a larger conflict. While people do not generally like to experience battles, this has become a way of life today. We have to battle from childhood until death to become successful. Indeed, we have to battle through the challenges we face daily.

I'm from a family of six siblings, and I was the last of them all. As a child it was a battle to wake up early in the morning and get ready for school when I was enjoying my sleep. My mom, or sometimes my older brothers and sisters, would come and wake me up. I would say, "I don't want to get up," but I had to because education was a part of my future preparation for life. As a youth growing up, the battle I faced was to keep focused on what I had to do and to carry out responsibilities given to me, such as cleaning the house or helping in the kitchen. This was a battle for me because I would have preferred to be with my mates, hanging out with them.

People fight various kinds of battles to enhance their lives. These battles range from the individual level to the collective level of a nation battling for its values, principles, and way of life. Let's look at how countries fight to define their way of life. For example, consider the United States of America's "battle" for a way of life.

> The American way of life is an expression that refers to a national call that adheres to principles of life, liberty and the pursuit of happiness. It has connection to the American dream which affirms the supreme value and dignity of the individual; for he is never to rest but is always to be striving to "get ahead"; it defines an ethic of self-reliance, merit, and

character, and judges by achievement: "Deeds, not creeds" are what count.³

But how many Americans are able to achieve this dream and standard of living and therefore "win" this battle? At least some are pessimistic about the results.

> Most American people can see that the government serves the interests of corporations and the rich. It is true that capitalist ideology still holds a powerful influence over many people, like the idea of the "American Dream", that if you work hard, you can raise your standard of living. But this idea is beginning to crack under the pressure of Corporate America's unprecedented attacks on working peoples' living standards, especially the middle class.⁴

And so there is an internal battle between what the systems have set out for people to attain and what individuals can in reality attain. The same can be said of other continents, such as Australia, Africa, Europe, and Asia, and so the struggle to win individual battles as well as corporate ones is a global concern.

Before mankind became involved in these battles, there was a battle that took place in the heavens between Lucifer and the archangel Michael. Something had occurred in heaven that needed fixing. What was this? Let us see what the history book from God says.

> How you are fallen from heaven, O Lucifer, son of the morning! How you are cut down to the ground, you who weakened the nations! For you have said in your heart: I will ascend into heaven. I will exalt my throne above the star of God; I will also sit on the mount of the congregation on the farthest sides of the north. I will ascend above the heights of the clouds. I will be like the most high. (Isaiah 14:12–14)

We see that Lucifer became proud and exalted himself above God. This caused the war that broke out in heaven.

> And war broke out in heaven: Michael and his angels fought with the dragon; and the dragon and his angels fought, but they did not prevail, nor was a place found for them in heaven any longer. So the great dragon was cast out, that serpent of old, called the Devil and Satan, who deceives the whole world; he was cast to the earth [universe], and his angels were cast out with him. (Revelation 12:7–9)

The archangel Michael is the angel in charge of war, and he successfully contained the situation in heaven against another archangel, namely, Lucifer. Lucifer decided to exalt himself above God, the Creator. Michael was loyal to his Creator and fought against Lucifer, who was rebelling against God. It is important to note the disposal site—where Lucifer and his demons with him were cast out from the presence of God. The

Word of God says they were cast "to the earth" [universe] (Revelation 12:9). This is the same earth [universe] we see in Genesis 1:2 but *not* the earth God created in Genesis 1:10 for mankind to possess.

God's plan was to make mankind in His own image and provide a place for them to live here on earth. However, God had to sort out this heavenly conflict before creating mankind. After the successful containment of the conflict, Lucifer and his demons possessed the earth [universe], as indicated by Genesis 1:2. Lucifer and his demons are now referred to as darkness. Darkness had already taken over the face of the place called the "deep," and the rest of that place was water. This was the result of that first battle that took place before mankind was created by God.

Darkness occupied the deep, and it would have been an injustice to us if God had created the earth we live in and left it under the darkness. Therefore, God had to create light, which is the opposite of, and the antidote to, darkness. What are we saying then? When Lucifer fell from heaven, along with one-third of the angels, whom we now call demons, he fell on this place Moses called the earth [universe] in Genesis 1:2 (Revelation 12:9). This is why the Bible records that darkness was on the face of the deep (Genesis 1:2). Again, this was not yet the earth we live on; it was a deep, and it was occupied by water.

The Bible also gives us a scenario to help us understand the earth's darkness and light, and it centers on the Devil, who is our accuser before God. If there was a battle before mankind was created, that means there is still a battle going on that mankind is largely ignorant of and needs to awaken to. This is why when the Devil was thrown to the earth [universe], there was a woe pronounced upon the earth but rejoicing in heaven.

> Then I heard a loud voice saying in heaven, "Now salvation, and strength, and the kingdom of our God, and the power of His Christ have come, for the accuser of our brethren, who accused them before our God day and night, has been cast down. And they overcame him by the blood of the Lamb and by the word of their testimony, and they did not love their lives to the death. Therefore rejoice O heavens, and you who dwell in them! Woe to the inhabitants of the earth and the sea! For the devil has come down to you, having great wrath, because he knows that he has a short time." (Revelation 12:10–12)

This battle can be won only by the blood of the Lamb of God, Jesus Christ, and not by our ability and technology. This account helps us see that battles existed before and they are still in full force. The challenges we face today represent different kinds of battles we have to endure for various reasons. Often we find ourselves fighting battles that are not rational at all. Later, when we take a look back at the battles we've been fighting, we will see what a waste our efforts were.

The battles we face begin somewhere, and this is why we should always stop and ask ourselves some questions before going into any battle: Where is this battle coming from? What is the purpose of this battle? What does this battle involve? Who is affected by this battle? What are the benefits of engaging in this battle? By the time we decide to go to battle it should be clear that the results will bring pride and honor to us, our family, our friends, and our nation.

Look at a physical battle fought between two nations. Before the Israelites went to fight the people living in Canaan, Moses first sent spies to the land.

> Moses . . . said to them, "Go up this way into the South, and go up to the mountains, and see what the land is like: whether the people who dwell in it are strong or weak, few or many; whether the land they dwell in is good or bad; whether the cities they inhabit are like camps or strongholds; whether the land is rich or poor; and whether there are forests there or not." (Numbers 13:17–20)

Let us jump to verse 27 to get the report from the spies.

> "We went to the land where you sent us. It truly flows with milk and honey, and this is its fruit. Nevertheless the people who dwell in the land are strong; the cities are fortified and very large; moreover we saw the descendants of Anak there. The

Amalekites dwell in the land of the South; the Hittites, the Jebusites, and the Amorites dwell in the mountains; and the Canaanites dwell by the sea and along the banks of the Jordan." Then Caleb quieted the people before Moses, and said, "Let us go up at once and take possession, for we are well able to overcome it." But the men who had gone up with him said, "We are not able to go up against the people, for they are stronger than we." And they gave the children of Israel a bad report of the land which they had spied out, saying, "The land through which we have gone as spies is a land that devours its inhabitants, and all the people whom we saw in it are men of great stature. There we saw the giants (the descendants of Anak came from the giants); and we were like grasshoppers in our own sight, and so we were in their sight." (Numbers 13:27–33)

The ten spies said Israel was unable to possess the land. Why? Because, they said, "We were like grasshoppers in our own sight, and so we were in their sight" (Numbers 13:33). The question I always ask is this: "Were the ten spies lying?" The answer is no. They were speaking the truth. The people of the land were in fact strong and like giants. On the other hand, Caleb said, "Let us go up at once and take possession, for we are well able to overcome it" (verse 30). Caleb saw that the Lord had given Israel favor to possess the land. Was Caleb also speaking the truth? The answer is yes. What we do when we are faced with a battle matters. We can say the battle is over our head and opt to quit as the ten spies did, or we can brace ourselves and say that with God as our Helper, we will overcome. Moses' sending the spies to spy out the land was essential for Israel to know the military power of their enemy, but it was not meant to discourage them with their disabilities and incompetence.

Before an army goes out to battle, they prepare themselves to make sure they have full information on their enemy. They want to know how strong their enemies are, where they are located, who their enemies' allies are, and what weapons they have. In the same way, we also have to gather information when we have an individual battle. Understanding the battles we have to fight in our lives will help us become more effective and efficient in our undertakings. The battles we face will vary based on the different situations and circumstances we encounter, but the battles discussed below are very common.

1.1.1 The Battle of Pride

King Nebuchadnezzar was a proud Babylonian king who had an encounter with the living God. Let us look at what happened to him when he was well established in his kingdom.

> At the end of the twelve months he was walking about the royal palace of Babylon. The king spoke, saying, "Is not this great Babylon, that I have built for a royal dwelling by my mighty power and for the

honor of my majesty?" While the word was still in the king's mouth, a voice fell from heaven: "King Nebuchadnezzar, to you it is spoken: the kingdom has departed from you! And they shall drive you from men, and your dwelling shall be with the beasts of the field. They shall make you eat grass like oxen; and seven times shall pass over you, until you know that the Most High rules in the kingdom of men, and gives it to whomever He chooses." (Daniel 4:29-32)

Previously the king of Babylon had a dream, which was explained to him by the prophet Daniel. It concerned the king's pride and what would happen to him as a result. Can we relate to this event recorded by the prophet Daniel? This account helps us understand that pride is a battle in our lives we have to fight, making sure it does not destroy us as it did Nebuchadnezzar, the king of Babylon. Note what followed the proclamation from heaven: "That very hour the word was fulfilled concerning Nebuchadnezzar; he was driven from men and ate grass like oxen; his body was wet with the dew of heaven till his hair had grown like eagles' feathers and his nails like birds' claws" (Daniel 4:33).

Pride and self-conceit are sins that especially plague those who are in authority and possess great wealth. We are good at taking to ourselves the glory due God. This certainly was the case with the king of Babylon. Nebuchadnezzar's proud words were still in his mouth when the word came from God. What happened? The understanding and memory of the king were taken away, and all the powers of his proud soul were broken. God resists the proud. Nebuchadnezzar thought himself to be more than a man, but God justly made him less than a man. God's power cannot be resisted. King Solomon wrote, "Pride goes before destruction, and a haughty spirit before a fall" (Proverbs 16:18). When we think of ourselves more highly than we ought to think, we are walking in pride and we have a haughty spirit, and God resists these attitudes. We sometimes believe we have given ourselves life that we are in control of our lives and can say and do whatever we want. Let us learn from the king of Babylon.

When we think about battles today, we can see that most battles are fought because of pride. Pride does not take into account who is affected. It is not concerned with what the warlords call "collateral damage" (as long as it suits you or as long as it suits your country, that's it and all, is well). The battle of pride is a battle mankind cannot win without God. It will only create conflict. God resists the proud and gives grace to the humble. When our heart is lifted up in pride that means it is lifted up as a god. There is only one God, however, and He will surely bring us down in humiliation or ruin. We need to make sure pride does not bring our lives down. This is a battle we need to win.

1.1.2 The Battle of Power

Power is something human beings like to have. Power brings an unexplained feeling that is different from pride, but at the same time it cultivates pride. As a result pride usually becomes a way of life for the one with power. This is why people will do everything in their power to remain in the state of power. The king of Egypt found it hard to understand the message Moses and Aaron brought from the Lord God of Israel. Remember what Moses and Aaron told Pharaoh: "'thus says the LORD God of Israel: "Let My people go, that they may hold a feast to Me in the wilderness."' And Pharaoh said, 'Who is the LORD THAT I should obey His voice to let Israel go? I do not know the LORD, nor will I let Israel go'" (Exodus 5:1–2). As in the case of Nebuchadnezzar, God had to show Pharaoh that He was the omnipotent God, the all-powerful God, and His chosen people were the Israelites. This was not up for debate. The one and only almighty God would set His people free from the terror of darkness.

    Pharaoh, being a lord himself, could not take instructions from another Lord—especially one he could not see. As you read the account recorded in the book of Exodus, you will understand how controlling power can become. People who have it will risk their lives to keep it! If we look at Africa and the power struggles and violence there, we will again see and understand the control power has over people who seek it. Power in itself is a good thing, but too much of it, when possessed by a few, can lead to great evil. This is why Jesus taught His disciples, "Whoever desires to become great among you, let him be your servant. And whoever desires to be first among you, let him be your slave just as the Son of Man did not come to be served, but to serve, and to give His life a ransom for many" (Matthew 20:26-28).

1.1.3 The Battle of Wealth

As with power, wealth by itself is also good. Adam and Eve were the first wealthy people on earth. When they began to focus on themselves and took their eyes off God, their Creator, they fell from grace to disgrace.

It is good for us to have wealth. However, when wealth cultivates pride within us, which it has the power to do; it becomes a huge problem that affects mankind's relationship with the Creator. We see this in a parable Jesus spoke to His listeners.

> "The ground of a certain rich man yielded plentifully. And he thought within himself, saying, 'What shall I do, since I have no room to store my crops?' So he said, 'I will do this: I will pull down my barns and build greater, and there I will store all my crops and my goods. And I will say to my soul, "Soul, you have many goods laid up for many years; take your ease; eat, drink, and be merry."' But God said to him, 'Fool! This night your soul will be required of you; then whose will those things be which you have provided?' So is he who lays up treasure for himself, and is not rich toward God." (Luke 12:16-21)

The people of the world receive some degree of happiness and comfort from accumulating the wealth of this world. But the things of the world will not satisfy and fulfill the desires and emptiness of our soul. We see in this parable the omnipotent God at work on the earth. Those who fail to regard the providence of God will be judged immediately, as in the case of this rich man. When we put ourselves in the driver's seat, we always go wrong. Things happen, and the more we try to fix them, the more the problems escalate. Even if things go well for a while, soon we are again under fire in the battle of life. If we are speaking like this rich man, it is time to stop and give proper regard to the providence of God over the earth. When the rich man got a bumper harvest, instead of thanking God, the first thing that came to his mind was the question, what shall I do now? It was folly for him to think of himself and not make any other use of his plenty. The judgment of such people is miserable and comes upon them suddenly.

1.1.4 The Battle of Submission

The world today has sought to do away with the concept of submission and even the word *submit*. Children no longer submit to their parents, wives no longer submit to their husbands, students no longer submit to their teachers, and so on. Many people believe submission would deprive them of assertiveness. It is interesting to see where we are heading. Think about a world full of chiefs with no subordinates! On the contrary, Jesus set an example when He was submissive to His Father's will. He said, "Father, if it is Your will, take this cup away from Me; nevertheless not My will, but Yours, be done" (Luke 22:42). We can learn so much from this account of Jesus' submission to the Father. This was the prayer He prayed in the garden of Gethsemane just before His arrest and crucifixion. Jesus is seen as meek and lowly of heart. His words paint a vivid picture of what was going through His mind. Undoubtedly, Jesus anticipated great pain in His body. In addition, knowing He was innocent and undeserving of death, He had to resist the urge to break faith and sin against God's will for His life. Perhaps the most dreaded burden of all was He knew that He was going to be cut off from God and has to bear the sin of all mankind alone. Yet Jesus by faith consciously chose to submit to God the Father.

What an example! Submission enables us to be humble and not puffed up. Many are submissive to their bosses because of the paycheck. Sometimes they would like to stand up to their bosses and walk in disobedience, but if they do so, they might lose their jobs. Therefore, on the outside they pretend they love what they do, while inside they are on fire. If such conflict within us continues for long, it will affect not only us but also our families. We need to learn submission.

When we arrived in Australia and began to fellowship with a church, the pastor said to me, "Australians do not like to be told what to do." If this statement is true, then God help us! How many Australians are saved? How many know our Lord Jesus Christ? Submission is a vital part of life, and it is a tool we can use against self, pride, and power. Indeed, we have to submit to God to be saved.

1.1.5 The Battle of Lust

What is lust? Lust is "an intense or unrestrained sexual craving. It is an overwhelming desire or craving for power, sex or life."[5]

We can add that lust also is a spiritual matter; it is a desire within us or before our eyes, whether for a person or for a thing, that often is sustained for a long period of time. Lust is a battle that all mankind fights. And how many of us win the battle against lust? Not many. Here is what Jesus told His listeners concerning lust: "But I say to you that whoever looks at a woman to lust for her has already committed adultery with her in his heart. If your right eye causes you to sin, pluck it out and cast it from you; for it is more profitable for you that one of your members perish, than for your whole body to be cast into hell" (Matthew 5:28–29).

Victory over the lust of the eye is crucial, and that victory often requires us to take a long and painful path. But we need to win over that desire of the heart, for lust leads us contrary to God's will for our lives. We need to present this battle to God and ask Him to help us because by ourselves we cannot make it. We live in a world where immorality has become a way of life, and the sky is the limit to this abomination. Those who engage in immorality are accountable for their actions to God. At the same time, we have to brace ourselves for what is to come and guard our eyes, which open the door to lust. Thank God there is mercy for all the divine requirements, and the Spirit of grace will cover us. This is why before Jesus Christ ascended into heaven, He prayed for His disciples, saying, "I do not pray that You should take them out of the world, but that You should keep them from the evil one. They are not of the world, just as I am not of the world" (John 17:15–16).

As we said before, all of mankind goes through this battle of lust, and most lose the battle. Why? We often refuse to let go of our desires. Jesus said, "If your right eye causes you to sin, pluck it out and cast it from you." Does this mean we should physically pluck out our eyes? No. The revelation here is that we must stop looking at the thing that causes us to lust. Don't even go near it. Keep away from it. If we refuse to disconnect ourselves from lust, we will become slaves to it. Let us consider the effects of lust in a sad account from the Bible.

> After this Absalom the son of David had a lovely sister, whose name was Tamar; and Amnon the son of David loved her. Amnon was so distressed over his sister Tamar that he became sick; for she was a virgin. And it was improper for Amnon to do anything to her. But Amnon had a friend whose name was Jonadab the son of Shimeah, David's brother. Now Jonadab was a very crafty man. And he said to him, "Why are you, the king's son, becoming thinner day after day? Will you not tell me?"

Amnon said to him, "I love Tamar, my brother Absalom's sister."

So Jonadab said to him, "Lie down on your bed and pretend to be ill. And when your father comes to see you, say to him, 'Please let my sister Tamar come and give me food, and prepare the food in my sight, that I may see it and eat it from her hand.'" Then Amnon lay down and pretended to be ill; and when the king came to see him, Amnon said to the king, "Please let Tamar my sister come and make a couple of cakes for me in my sight, that I may eat from her hand."

And David sent home to Tamar, saying, "Now go to your brother Amnon's house, and prepare food for him." So Tamar went to her brother Amnon's house; and he was lying down. Then she took flour and kneaded it, made cakes in his sight, and baked the cakes. And she took the pan and placed them out before him, but he refused to eat. Then Amnon said, "Have everyone go out from me." And they all went out from him. Then Amnon said to Tamar, "Bring the food into the bedroom that I may eat from your hand." And Tamar took the cakes which she had made, and brought them to Amnon her brother in the bedroom. Now when she had brought them to him to eat, he took hold of her and said to her, "Come, lie with me, my sister."

But she answered him, "No, my brother, do not force me, for no such thing should be done in Israel. Do not do this disgraceful thing! And I, where could I take my shame? And as for you, you would be like one of the fools in Israel. Now therefore, please speak to the king; for he will not withhold me from you." However, he would not heed her voice; and being stronger than she, he forced her and lay with her.

Then Amnon hated her exceedingly, so that the hatred with which he hated her was greater than the love with which he had loved her. And Amnon said to her, "Arise, be gone!"

So she said to him, "No, indeed! This evil of sending me away is worse than the other that you did to me."

But he would not listen to her. (2 Samuel 13:1–16)

The power of lust! How many of us can identify with the account we just read? We lust after someone or something. When we get the object of our lust and have used it, we have no use for it anymore! This is what lust is all about. Lust steals our life and destroys it. This is why we need to ask questions that will help us avoid lust. If we realize we are controlled by lust, we need to humble ourselves and get help. This topic is discussed again in chapter 5 under the subtitle "Personal Evaluation."

1.1.6 The Battle to Love and Not Hate

When I was attending the Illawarra TAFE College in New South Wales, Australia, I got into a conversation with one of my classmates during a lunch break. She was a Christian, and we began to share about the Christian faith. She said to me, "I want to love those who have hurt me, but I can't." Many of us are carrying hate within us, and it has become excess baggage in our lives. It is weighing us down. We even confess, as my classmate did, that we are Christians—Christians with hate and unforgiveness in our hearts! In saying this, we are not making ourselves your judge. We are simply revealing what a battle it is to love those who abuse and hurt us. Listen to what Jesus said: "But I say to you who hear: Love your enemies, do good to those who hate you, bless those who curse you, and pray for those who spitefully use you" (Luke 6:27–28). Marriages, families, and friends are experiencing this battle between love and hate right now. It is tearing them apart. We find ourselves often at the "hate" end of the line rather than the "love" end. This means we are losing the battle to love. Let us see how the Bible describes true love.

> Love suffers long and is kind; love does not envy; love does not parade itself, is not puffed up; does not behave rudely, does not seek its own, is not provoked, thinks no evil; does not rejoice in iniquity, but rejoices in the truth; bears all things, believes all

things, hopes all things, endures all things. Love never fails. (1 Corinthians 13:4–8)

As I was speaking with a friend, we were looking at the book of Ephesians, where the Word of God says, "Husbands love your wives" (Ephesians 5:25). I said to her, "Sometimes we need to ask wives and husbands what love is to them." I believe people have many views of what love is. When someone defines love as "my husband taking me out and taking me shopping," then that person sees the love of her husband only through cash or certain acts. She does not really understand what love is. This is why we have so many divorces today: People do not understand what love is.

If your husband believes in you, hopes in you, and endures all that is put on him because of you, then he is a man of love. Many wives, especially in the West, believe love is receiving a bouquet of flowers from their husbands. What happens when the flowers dry up and die? Does this mean your husband's love for you has died? If a woman says to her husband, "If you love me, then buy that car for me," that wife does not know what love is. She will not appreciate love because her eyes will always be wanting. We need to win the battle of love today. Love never seeks its own to the hurt of others or to the neglect of others. It even prefers the welfare of others to its own advantage. Does this divine love dwell in our hearts? Has this principle guided us into good behavior toward all people? Are we willing to lay aside our selfish aims and show love to others? This is a call to diligence and prayer.

1.1.7 The Battle of Peace

We all need peace, not only in our lives, but also in the world in which we live. We need peace. This is another battle mankind is fighting. The harder we search for peace, the further away from peace we seem to get. This is often because we are looking for peace in the wrong places. There is a false peace we can give ourselves that comes from the things of this world. The world always offers different options, but there is just one way to real peace: through our Lord Jesus Christ. He said, "Peace I leave with you, My peace I give to you; not as the world gives do I give to you. Let not your heart be troubled, neither let it be afraid" (John 14:27).

Today the world yearns for this precious jewel called peace, but they cannot find it. This is because the way to true peace is not broad but narrow, and there are few who walk this road. True peace of mind in life is a virtue we need to live out in this troubled world. All over the world, people are looking for true peace, and this peace has been given to us by our Lord Jesus Christ. What a blessing it is to be a child of God and experience peace of mind in this life of war! If you are not experiencing this peace as a Christian, you need to ask yourself why. If you earnestly examine yourself before God, you will discover the problem, get it fixed, and enjoy peace in Jesus Christ.

1.1.8 The Battle of Greed

I think we can say that greed has already won over mankind and has become a way of life in today's world. What a shame it is that greed is operating and flourishing in our world! To so many people, money is god, and they worship it. There is nothing they do without thinking, "What am I getting out of this deal?" The Bible records the consequences of one man's greed in the Old Testament. His actions alone made the children of Israel lose a battle to the small city of Ai.

> But the children of Israel committed a trespass regarding the accursed things, for Achan the son of Carmi, the son of Zabdi, the son of Zerah, of the tribe of Judah, took of the accursed things; so the anger of the LORD burned against the children of Israel. … And Achan answered Joshua and said, "Indeed I have sinned against the LORD God of Israel, and this is what I have done: When I saw among the spoils a beautiful Babylonian garment, two hundred shekels of silver, and a wedge of gold weighing fifty shekels, I coveted them and took them. And there they are, hidden in the earth in the midst of my tent, with the silver under it."
>
> So Joshua sent messengers, and they ran to the tent; and there it was, hidden in his tent, with the silver under it. And they took them from the midst of the tent, brought them to Joshua and to all the children of Israel, and laid them out before the LORD.

> Then Joshua, and all Israel with him, took Achan the son of Zerah, the silver, the garment, the wedge of gold, his sons, his daughters, his oxen, his donkeys, his sheep, his tent, and all that he had, and they brought them to the Valley of Achor. And Joshua said, "Why have you troubled us? The LORD will trouble you this day." So all Israel stoned him with stones; and they burned them with fire after they had stoned them with stones.
>
> Then they raised over him a great heap of stones, still there to this day. So the LORD turned from the fierceness of His anger. (Joshua 7:1, 20–26)

The love of money is the root of all sorts of evil (1 Timothy 6:10), and has blinded us to the extent that our relationships and friendships are businesslike, making it difficult to find real friends.

Greed will cause you to do the wrong things in life. You may be enjoying the fruits of greed right now because you have not been caught, but it will catch up with you, as it caught up with Achan. There is nothing hidden from God, whether you believe in God or not (Hebrews 4:13). Greed is an enemy to mankind, and those who walk in it will be condemned.

Achan believed he could hide from God. The children of Israel were instructed not to take anything from the city of Jericho. Everything was to be destroyed. Because of greed Achan disobeyed the word of God. Whenever we disobey God's orders, consequences always follow, as we see in the case of Achan. He was destroyed with his family, along with all of his possessions. If we allow greed to control our lives, we become slaves to it—and this is exactly what we see today. The world stock market is a center of greed. A stock market controlled by man is a market that manifests the power of greed. Indeed, man seeks to manipulate the markets and hide from others the truth that greed motivates him and drives the market.

1.1.9 The Battle of Deception

Deception is a way of life today. We will be looking at deception intensely in the chapters to come, but for now let us look at a parable Jesus told His listeners. Note the deception of one of the characters.

> "But what do you think? A man had two sons, and he came to the first and said, 'Son, go, work today in my vineyard.' He answered and said, 'I will not,' but afterward he regretted it and went. Then he came to the second and said likewise. And he answered and said, 'I go, sir,' but he did not go. Which of the two did the will of his father?" They said to Him, "The first." (Matthew 21:28–31)

We realize that even our children deceive us. In fact, this is another battle mankind has lost; we have chosen deception and have made it a way of life. How many times do people say,

"I will do it" and then they do not? When we pretend we will do something and do not carry it out, we have lied and become deceivers, just as the second son in Jesus' parable who told his father he would go but did not. We can decide not to engage in deception if our "yes" is "yes" and our "no" is "no." We should not try to be the savior of the world. We should do what we can and not promise to do what we cannot or are not willing to do. At times, out of the goodness of our hearts, we may not want to say no. However, if we are struggling and complaining about all the work that is stressing us, we are breaking down our body and may find ourselves unable to perform the task.

1.1.10 The Battle of Health

Health is a battle that mankind constantly fights. But starting early in history with traditional medicine and progressing through experimental trials and modern medicine, great advancement has been made in the health sector. For example, let's look at some of the breakthroughs that have come in the treatment of cancer.

In an article titled "breakthroughs in the battle against Cancer," the National Foundation for Cancer Research (NFCR) reports it has made much progress over the past forty years in the battle against cancer.

> Since 1973, NFCR has provided more than $300 million to fund cancer research and prevention education. Although the world

still has a long way to go in terms of cancer treatment, NFCR has helped more than 11 million cancer survivors living in the United States. NFCR has allowed some of the world's brightest scientists to take initial steps toward breakthrough discoveries, laying the groundwork for the development of many of todays most innovative and effective cancer therapies. NFCR is making a difference in the lives of millions of cancer patients and their families' worldwide.[6]

Despite all the advancement in research, people are still dying of different forms of cancer, so individuals' battles with cancer continue. Today health has become an issue for most of us. Because of this, our doctors advise us to eat certain foods or to take up some exercises or other practices that will help keep us healthy. But, to God be the glory, we can also stand on His words and experience good health. The prophet Isaiah said of Jesus, "But He was wounded for our transgressions, He was bruised for our iniquities; the chastisement for our peace was upon Him, and by His stripes we are healed (Isaiah 53:5). God also promised the children of Israel (and by extension, us) protection from all sickness and diseases. He said, "If you diligently heed the voice of the Lord your God and do what is right in His sight, give ear to His commandments and keep all His statutes, I will put none of the diseases on you which I have brought on the Egyptians. For I am the Lord who heals you" (Exodus 15:26).

At times God may allow the Devil to bring diseases to us with the hope that we will resist the Devil and God will be glorified. This is what happened to righteous Job. Let us see what Satan did to Job's health and the effect this had on his wife.

> So Satan went out from the presence of the LORD, and struck Job with painful boils from the sole of his foot to the crown of his head. And he took for himself a potsherd with which to scrape himself while he sat in the midst of the ashes. Then his wife said to him, "Do you still hold fast to your integrity? Curse God and die!" But he said to her, "You speak as one of the foolish women speaks. Shall we indeed accept good from God, and shall we not accept adversity?" In all these Job did not sin with his lips. (Job 2:7–10)

What a great honor it is for God to know us by name! The account of Job reveals many of the hidden things behind what happens to us here on earth. One servant of God says, "The record currently playing in your life in the physical had been passed in the spiritual a long time ago, at times even before you were born." This account of Job shows us God knows His children and He protects those who are His. In order for the enemy to attack us, he needs permission from our Father God. Job was a man of integrity, and he feared God and shunned evil. The Devil believed that by striking Job's flesh with sickness, he could cause Job to sin against God. However, Job held on to his integrity. Even his wife said to him, "Curse God and die" (Job 2:9), but this did not move him. What a man of faith he was, a man who truly loved God for who God is, not for what God gives!

How many of us today can stand on God's side as Job did when trials come our way? How many of us have cursed God because of what happened to us or to our loved ones? How many of us embrace the flesh and deny the spirit? Job said to his wife, "You speak as one of the foolish women" (Job 2:10). Job fought the battle of health, and he rightly believed his life was in God's hand and God had the power to do what He so pleased. The most important thing a child of God has is his or her integrity. Without integrity, we are nobodies. We can pretend we are children of God, but we will know within us that we have lost the battle. Because Job held on to his integrity, he overcame, and God restored his good health and doubled his wealth.

The above battles are just a few examples. There may be other battles you can name or think about that we are engaged in, such as drugs and alcohol, immorality, anger, unforgiveness, lying, grief, and so on. We are all engaged in battles. The question is who is winning?

1.2 Existing Powers over the Earth

"Darkness was on the face of the deep," Genesis 1:2 tells us. Darkness has been in existence since the beginning, even before God called forth the earth we live on. In verse 1 of Genesis 1, the Word of God describes God as the

Creator of the heavens and the earth, and verse 2 gives us details on the display of God's ingenious power. Darkness occupied the deep, but it would have been an injustice to mankind if God had created the earth we live on and left it in the darkness, as we stated earlier. Therefore, God created light, which is the opposite of, and antidote to, darkness. Darkness had possessed the deep. The Spirit of God had to operate over the waters, and God created light from over the water. This was the first day. God took a whole day to create just one thing: light. When the *order of darkness* and the *order of light* were in place, then God went on to create and call forth our present earth: "And God called the dry land Earth" (Genesis 1:10). Friends, this is a great revelation, that the "earth" [universe] in Genesis 1:2 is different from the "Earth" in Genesis 1:10 but is the same as the "earth" [universe] in Revelation 12:9. The "Earth" in Genesis 1:10 is the same as the "earth" in Revelation 12:12. God, who created mankind, did not hide this information from us. The question is how many of us read God's Word and understands it?

    The diversity of life shows the uniqueness of the Creator of the universe and of mankind. Often we believe our opinion matters when it comes to God, the one and only Creator, who made all things. Our opinion does not matter, that is the truth. The apostle Paul asked, "Will their unbelief make the faithfulness of God without effect? (Romans 3:3). Certainly not! Individually, we may have our opinions on our country's or other countries' domestic and international affairs. Will they change their policies because of how you think or feel about them? The answer is no. For example, you might not be happy with paying your taxes or passing a driving test before you can be allowed to drive a car alone. However, these policies will remain in place despite how you feel about them. Yes, the big guns play the cards, not according to equality but according to their own interests and benefits. All around us we see this reality. Those in authority make decisions they believe will benefit the country and them. The masses have to accept it, whether it's going to benefit them or not. They have to accept it because it is the policy of the day or for the time. This pattern originated with the Creator of mankind, and His name is Jehovah God. We may choose to believe the Bible or not, but the truth is, it doesn't matter whether you and I believe in the Bible and in Jesus Christ or not. Our belief or disbelief will not change the fact that there are existing powers over the earth we live on.

    Being a believer from childhood, I remember my mom taking me to church. My worship to God at the time was to run up and down in the church whenever I had the chance to do so. I would dance and sing what I understood at the time. I enjoyed it, and it was always good. Even when I had to be put in a seat forcefully it was still good. This training at church helped discipline and cultivate the character within me today. As I grew up and began to read the Bible, the Word of God, for myself, and as preachers preached the Word of God, I always understood Genesis 1:2–5 to be related to the earth's night and day.

> The earth [universe] was without form, and void; and darkness was on the face of the deep. And the Spirit of God was hovering over the face of the waters. Then God said, "Let there be light"; and there was light. And God saw the light that it was good; and God divided the light from the darkness. God called the light Day, and the darkness He called Night. So the evening and the morning were the first day. (Genesis 1:2–5)

I believed this referred to the night and day we experience, our twenty-four-hour days. Nevertheless, in November 2012, the Holy Spirit opened my eyes concerning these verses, and I exclaimed, "Wow! Is this real? Am I really seeing what I'm seeing?" I could not believe what I was seeing for the very first time in my life! Yes, I could not believe it, but there it was. I was looking at a vital revelation that could help me—and I believe other believers—to have a better understanding of the Word of God and of the enemy fighting against God's children.

Genesis 1:1 reveals God as the Creator of heavens and the earth [universe], as we stated earlier: "In the beginning God created the heavens and the earth [universe]." Then verse 2 begins to tell us how God created the heavens and the earth [universe]. In Genesis 1:2–3 God pronounces two distinct orders that were in existent before He created the earth we live in and everything within it. "The earth [universe] was without form, and void; and darkness was on the face of the deep. And the Spirit of God was hovering over the face of the waters," verse 2 tells us. At the time, the first earth [universe] was not much of an earth because of its emptiness.

What we need to capture here are two things. First, darkness was upon the face of the first earth [universe], and beside the deep there was only water. Second, the Spirit of God was hovering over the waters. Because of the darkness that had possessed the deep, God had to make light first. And out of nothing, God made something. We know when Lucifer was defeated, he fell to the first earth [universe] and possessed the earth's deep (as we saw in the section "Battle in Heaven"), leaving God no place to stand except upon water. If there is no place in our lives on which God can stand, then there can be no calling forth of light. That is why the Word of God says it is not by works that we are saved but by grace through faith (Ephesians 2:8). We need to give room to Jesus Christ in our lives to make something out of nothing. "Then God said, 'Let there be light'; and there was light" (Genesis 1:3). The darkness upon the deep covered everything, and we know that darkness is the opposite of light. God is light.

God refused to call forth the dry land from the waters without having a balance. If there was darkness, there had to be light, which is the opposite of darkness. Knowing what the darkness was, God had to make sure there was something that could counteract the darkness. That is why in the garden of God, which is the garden of Eden, were both the Tree of the Knowledge of Good and Evil and the Tree of Life

(Genesis 2:9). Earth operates under these two orders: *light* and *darkness*. God, the Creator, has given us knowledge of this and the willpower to choose which of the orders we will exercise in and over our lives. This is the fourth order, and it is by this order mankind will be judged.

As discussed previously, our opinion on this matter of orders will not and cannot change God's commandment. We either fall in line or fall out. The decision is ours, not God's. You and I can play the blame game or reject God because of what is or what has happened to us or our family and friends. But that does not change God's commandment. We need to ask ourselves this: What power is operating in and over our lives?

There is an *order of darkness* over the earth and an *order of light* over the earth. God has declared it and revealed it to us, as He did to Adam in the Garden of Eden. When we have our own values and principles we live by, we become furious when someone tries to break them. If we can stand up for ourselves, how much more can God, who has given us that nature that makes us want to do something about what is happening in and around our lives, stand up for His principles? God is definitely going to stand up for Himself, whether we believe it or not. The *order of darkness* and the *order of light* exist over the earth, and God will stand up for the values and principles He has established and revealed to mankind through His Word. "The light shines in the darkness, and the darkness did not comprehend it" (John 1:5), John wrote. And the apostle Paul recorded this:

For you were once darkness, but now you are light in the Lord. Walk as children of light (for the fruit of the Spirit is in all goodness, righteousness, and truth), finding out what is acceptable to the Lord. And have no fellowship with the unfruitful works of darkness, but rather expose them. For it is shameful even to speak of those things which are done by them in secret. But all things that are exposed are made manifest by the light, for whatever makes manifest is light. Therefore He says: "Awake, you who sleep, Arise from the dead, and Christ will give you light." (Ephesians 5:8–14)

We can ask ourselves, "Why do these powers exist?" or "Why did God, who knew that darkness was a profanation to light, not get rid of the darkness?" or "What is this all about, and why are we the victims of the end result?" I can assure you these questions have crossed my mind, and I have tried to formulate answers for them, but at the end of the day, the answers formulated might or might not be the right ones. Nevertheless, I have come to know through my experience that truly there are powers that exist over us, namely, *light and darkness.*

As an African, I lived my entire adult life in Africa. I heard about practices that we know as witchcraft and other demonic manifestations in families and villages. As an adult man, I left Africa and came to Australia. Now I see these same powers manifesting at a different level, where people are their own gods. Will God's policy and rule of order change because of what we do or because of what we believe or do not believe? As we said before, no, it will not change God's policy. Neither will it change the fact that we have the willpower to choose which power operates over and in our lives—light or darkness.

It is interesting to note some believe they have both orders operating over and in their lives! What great confusion this creates because one order wants to be lord over the other. We need to choose one and not both. Hear Joshua's advice to the children of Israel.

> "And if it seems evil to you to serve the LORD, choose for yourselves this day whom you will serve, whether the gods which your fathers served that were on the other side of the River, or the gods of the Amorites, in whose land you dwell. But as for me and my house, we will serve the LORD." (Joshua 24:15)

1.3　The Earth's Creation and Man's Dominion

The psalmist wrote, "The fool has said in his heart, 'There is no God.' They are corrupt, they have done abominable works, there is none who does good" (Psalm 14:1).

I grew up as a child in the city of Monrovia, Liberia. Allow me to briefly highlight some background on this West African country.

Liberia is a republic on the west coast of Africa. It is bounded on the north by Guinea, on the east by Côte d'Ivoire, on the southwest by the Atlantic Ocean, and on the northwest by

Sierra Leone. Liberia's coastline measures about 560 kilometers. Its area is 111,369 square kilometers. Except for narrow, marshy lowland along the coast, Liberia is largely a hilly plateau. After Ethiopia, Liberia is Africa's oldest independent country. The only large city is Monrovia, the capital. The current population estimate is 3,556,000 with a density of 32 per square kilometer. Fifty-two percent of the people live in rural areas, while 48 percent live in urban areas. English is the official language. It and various pidgin tongues based on English are spoken by 30 percent of the population; most of the people speak African languages. There are also some Christians and some Muslims. Schooling is nominally compulsory for children up to the age of sixteen. About 40 percent of the people are literate. The national university, established in 1951, is in Monrovia. Most of Liberia's people live by subsistence farming.[7]

  I can remember clearly that all the people I knew in Liberia believed in some spiritual power that they worshiped. And that which people believed in is what kept them going. Being fortunate to travel through the other West African countries, I saw people there who also believed in some spiritual power that engulfed their lives. As an adult, I had an opportunity to travel to Australia, which brought me into contact with people who believe in something like science and others who believe in themselves as god.

  Have I become judgmental of this world? The answer is no. I believe every human being has the right to believe in whatever he or she chooses. The choices people have made again reveal our great diversity as human beings. I can assure you I have never been among the smartest people of our time, but I thank God for such people because they have invented cures for sicknesses and advanced our technology. I am interested in the research done by scientists who study life and death, for example, because it helps to reveal the Creator to mankind today. I believe anyone who rejects science, which is the study of living and non-living things, is rejecting God's knowledge, which He has placed in nature and in mankind. In fact, He prophesied that knowledge would increase in the end time. This is what he said to the prophet Daniel: "But you, Daniel, shut up the words, and seals the book until the time of the end; many shall run to and fro, and knowledge shall increase" (Daniel 12:4). However, anyone who believes science *is* God is rejecting the source of knowledge—that is, the true God—and this is plagiarism. Why? This is because it is worshipping the creature and not the Creator. God expects us to acknowledge Him and give Him the glory for the knowledge He has given us. This is what He says of Himself: "I am the LORD, that is My name; and My glory I will not give to another, Nor My praise to carved images" (Isaiah 42:8).

It is good that every human being has the freedom to believe in whatever he or she wants to believe in—religion, science, cults, witchcraft, self, and so on. But is that belief true? Is it genuine? Is it helpful? Does it edify? The Bible says, "All things are lawful for me, but not all things are helpful; all things are lawful for me, but not all things edify" (1 Corinthians 10:23). You don't have to believe this, but I can assure you that every human being has a basic life philosophy that formulates his or her beliefs, which in turn determines how the person relates to the world. Nevertheless, I share with you another way. King Solomon said, "The fear of the Lord is the beginning of wisdom, and the knowledge of the Holy One is understanding" (Proverbs 9:10).

    The Bible is the book that has lasted from age to age, and it is the best source of information when it comes to the formation of the earth. According to Genesis 1:1, God created the heavens and the earth. Verses 2 and following uncover the omnipotence of God as He spoke the present earth and heavens into existence. Let's hear Him.

> Then God said, "Let there be a firmament in the midst of the waters, and let it divide the waters from the waters." Thus God made the firmament, and divided the waters which were under the firmament from the waters which were above the firmament; and it was so. And God called the firmament Heaven. (Genesis 1:6–8)

    God then proceeded to create the earth and the sea.

> Then God said, "Let the waters under the heavens be gathered together into one place, and let the dry land appear"; and it was so. And God called the dry land Earth, and the gathering together of the waters

> He called Seas. And God saw that it was good. (Genesis 1:9–10)

The omnipotent God began to speak His plan into existence. He first commanded the waters to be gathered together and the land to appear. We may believe in a theory rather than believe in God and His work of creation, but questions will always exist with our theory simply because it is not right. It took only the word of God Almighty to bring forth all that we behold with our eyes today. And God saw that His work was good. We enjoy viewing the earth's natural scenery because of the Mastermind who spoke it into being.

God then proceeded to bring forth the plants.

> Then God said, "Let the earth bring forth grass, the herb that yields seed, and the fruit tree that yields fruit according to its kind, whose seed is in itself, on the earth"; and it was so. And the earth brought forth grass, the herb that yields seed according to its kind, and the tree that yields fruit, whose seed is in itself according to its kind. And God saw that it was good. (Genesis 1:11–12)

Then God created the sun, moon, and stars.

> Then God said, "Let there be lights in the firmament of the heavens to divide the day from the night; and let them be for signs and seasons, and for days and years; and let them be for lights in the firmament of

the heavens to give light on the earth"; and it was so. Then God made two great lights: the greater light to rule the day, and the lesser light to rule the night. He made the stars also. God set them in the firmament of the heavens to give light on the earth, and to rule over the day and over the night, and to divide the light from the darkness. And God saw that it was good. (Genesis 1:14–18)

In Genesis 1 there is a contrast between verses 2–5 and verses 14–18. Verses 2–5 speak of the darkness upon the deep, God speaking forth the light, and God separating the darkness from the light. Verse 16, however, says God then made two great lights: the greater light (the sun) to rule the day and the lesser light (the moon) to rule the night. The question, then, is this: What is the darkness that was upon the face of the deep, and what is the light God spoke forth in the beginning, before the sun and moon were created? This is what this book is all about: earth's darkness and light.

Then God made the fish, birds, and animals.

> Then God said, "Let the waters abound with an abundance of living creatures, and let birds fly above the earth across the face of the firmament of the heavens." So God created great sea creatures and every living thing that moves, with which the waters abounded, according to their kind, and every winged bird according to its

kind. And God saw that it was good. And God blessed them, saying, "Be fruitful and multiply, and fill the waters in the seas, and let birds multiply on the earth." So the evening and the morning were the fifth day. Then God said, "Let the earth bring forth the living creature according to its kind: cattle and creeping thing and beast of the earth, each according to its kind"; and it was so. And God made the beast of the earth according to its kind, cattle according to its kind, and everything that creeps on the earth according to its kind. And God saw that it was good. (Genesis 1:20-25)

God's provision for mankind continues. God called forth into existence the fish, fowl, beasts, and even insects. Who is like God? There is none like Jehovah! If God can speak these things into existence, we need to respect and fear the living God, who can destroy both the body and the soul (Matthew 10:28). He is worthy to be adored and worshiped!

Finally, God made man in His own image. Then God said, "Let Us make man in Our image, according to Our likeness; let them have dominion over the fish of the sea, over the birds of the air, and over the cattle, over all the earth and over every creeping thing that creeps on the earth." So God created man in His own image; in the image of God He created him; male and female He created them. (Genesis 1:26-27)

How wonderful is the Creator of heaven and the earth to mankind! I sometimes wonder how foolish we are when we begin to blame God for the bad things happening in our lives! Before God created mankind, He had already made all the provision mankind needed to live life. Because of our disobedience, we were put out of the presence of God and had to fend for ourselves. Instead of going back to God, our Creator, we went far away from Him. The question is why?

1.4   Prayer Guide for Chapter 1

The purpose of the prayer guide is to bring us into the reality of this life we are living on the earth. The more sincere we are as we pray, the better the results we will experience. We present four categories of prayers designed for people at various stages of belief or unbelief. The various stages are expressed as follows: (1) I do not believe there is a God; (2) I do not believe in one God and one way to God; (3) I believe in God but have backslidden; and (4) I believe and have faith in God.

1.4.1 I Do Not Believe There Is a God

If there is a God up there somewhere, I am speaking to You. You know I do not believe You exist or that You are God who created the heaven and the earth and are watching over this earth that I live in. If it is true that You created this world we live in and it belongs to You, I apologize for not knowing and believing in You. Even though I have heard about You from those who call themselves Christians, I have not believed this is true and I still do not believe you are the only almighty God. If you are the almighty God, I give my heart to You as I continue reading this book. Let Your will be done for me to know You are God and You are out there, wherever you are. Amen.

1.4.2 I Do Not Believe in One God and One Way to God

I have been praying to You whose image is in my sanctified place I have made for You. I know You are a god, and I believe in You. Nevertheless, if You are higher and greater than any god I serve, I want to know You; I want to believe in You and in You alone. Forgive me for being ignorant when I could have heard about You. If You are the one and only almighty God and there is none like You, through Your mercy, open the eyes of my understanding and my heart to know You and to accept You as my God. As you open my heart, enable me to denounce all other gods and accept You alone as my God. Amen.

1.4.3 I Believe in God but Have Backslidden

O, my soul says, why have I backslidden from God's free grace? Is it because God has not been fair to me? I called out to God when I needed Him, and He did not come through for me. Why is my soul still longing for You? O, God, why didn't You answer me? Where were You when I called? Where were You when my life was in checkmate? My pain, grief, and hurt remain. I see the scars and feel the shame. How can I come back to God and ask God to come back to me? The scars have made me lose my way; the shame I feel is all that remains. Who is to blame—the One who cares for me, or me? I realize I've been deceived into blaming my God who watches over me. O, my soul, shouts out and says, "I thirst for grace that quenches within, the grace that brings Christ to me, to be my Lord and save me from shame." My soul is obsessed with pain; the hurts have possessed my brain; the scars are right before my eyes, and still my soul longs to be set free. God of grace and God of mercy pardon me today, I plead; set me free in Jesus' name, that I may live life once again. Amen.

1.4.4 I Believe and Have Faith in God

Father God, I thank You for the grace You have given me, and I do not take it for granted. I believe You are the almighty God and the Creator of the heaven and the earth. I thank You for the opportunity to discover as I read this book the truth from Your Word that will help me understand this world I live in and be the servant You want me to be. In Jesus' name I pray. Amen.

CHAPTER TWO

THE GENESIS OF THE REIGNS OF KINGDOMS AND NATIONS

As the Creator and Designer of mankind, God set up kingdoms and nations. His providence is forever and is felt on the earth. Again, let us look at an account of King Nebuchadnezzar, when he spoke of his achievements without acknowledging God.

> The king spoke, saying, "Is not this great Babylon, that I have built for a royal dwelling by my mighty power and for the honour of my majesty?" (Daniel 4:30)

God's reaction to the king's pride was swift.

> While the word was still in the king's mouth, a voice fell from heaven: "King Nebuchadnezzar, to you it is spoken: the kingdom has departed from you! And they shall drive you from men, and your dwelling shall be with the beasts of the field. They shall make you eat grass like oxen; and seven times shall pass over you, until you know that the Most High rules in the kingdom of men, and gives it to whomever He chooses." (Daniel 4:31–32)

The effect of God's spoken word over the king was immediate.

> That very hour the word was fulfilled concerning Nebuchadnezzar; he was driven from men and ate grass like oxen; his body was wet with the dew of heaven till his hair had grown like eagles' feathers and his nails like birds' claws. (Daniel 4:33)

After this terrible encounter with the Almighty, King Nebuchadnezzar had a change of heart.

> And at the end of the time I, Nebuchadnezzar, lifted my eyes to heaven, and my understanding returned to me; and I blessed the Most High and praised and honoured Him who lives forever: For His dominion is an everlasting dominion, and His kingdom is from generation to generation (Daniel 4:34).

King Nebuchadnezzar ate grass like an animal because of his boast in himself. Here is an example of the battle of pride we discussed earlier.

The providence of God is forever, whether we believe it or not. The ancient nations knew they were to ascribe worship to God but they ascribed worship to other gods. Religion was a vital part of their existence. Let us look at two kingdoms and nations in times past and learn about their religious practices. We will look at the Persian Empire and ancient Rome.

It is very interesting to note how religion in the Persian Empire was deeply embedded in the law and how obedience to the law was related to God.

> The humaneness of the Persian rulers may have stemmed from the ethical religion founded by the prophet Zoroaster, who lived in the early sixth century B.C. Zoroaster sought to replace what he called "the lie"—ritualistic, idol-worshiping cults—with a religion centered on the sole god Ahura-Mazda ("Wise Lord"). This "father of Justice" demanded "good thoughts of the mind, good deeds of the hand, and good words of the tongue" from those who would attain paradise. The Magi revived many old gods as lesser deities, added much ritual, and replaced monotheism with dualism by transforming what Zoroaster had called the principle or spirit of evil into the powerful god Ahriman ... rival of Ahura-Mazda, "between which each man must choose for himself." Zoroastrian eschatology—"the doctrine of final things" such as the resurrection of the dead and a last judgment—influenced later Judaism. Following the Muslim conquest of Persia in the seventh century A.D., Zoroastrianism died out in its homeland. It exists today among the Parsees in India. In the Persian Empire, the law formed an essential part of religion, as one-third of their sacred

literature comprises Law in its various phases and spheres. Indeed Law in a wider sense coincided with Religion itself, for essentially the domain of Religion covered the universal field of Law. Hence it was that as Science too stood fully on the foundation of Law, Science constitutes the middle third of the Religious system of the Persians and forms an essential link between God and Man. In fact Law abidingness was one of the most meaningful of the names of the Supreme Being in the Persian Theology. So Aim of Law would be to promote Religion and Divinity in Mankind which would be furthered by the Spread of Learning and Knowledge among Men. The aim of Law is to further the Mighty Word of the All-Knowing Creator and to defeat Falsehood, and thus to compass in the end the immortal, the illustrious and the most Brilliant and Perfect Sovereignty of the Kingdom of God. This was possible, because Law-abidingness was deeply imbedded in the very nature of Humanity, and so the Divine Being has created the world and implanted man in it to live the Life of Righteous Progress; and this instinct of Law-abidingness is to prove useful and valuable in the distant end by means of knowledge and education, and discrimination and enlightenment and learning. Indeed the world would be the better and the happier if it followed this belief and practice of the ancient Persians.[1]

The next extract describes the beginnings of religion and its progression in ancient Rome before it became a Christian (Catholic) empire.

> Archaic Roman religion, at least concerning the gods, was made up not of written narratives, but rather of complex interrelations between gods and humans. Romans also believed that every person, place or thing had its own genius, or divine soul. During the Roman Republic, Roman religion was organized under a strict system of priestly offices, which were held by men of senatorial rank. Flamens took care of the cults of various gods, while augurs were trusted with taking the auspices. The sacred king took on the religious responsibilities of the deposed kings. In the Roman Empire, emperors were held to be gods, and the formalized imperial cult became increasingly prominent. As contact with the Greeks increased, the old Roman gods became increasingly associated with Greek gods. Thus, Jupiter was perceived to be the same deity as Zeus, Mars became associated with Ares, and Neptune with Poseidon. The Roman gods also assumed the attributes and mythologies of these Greek gods. The transferal of anthropomorphic qualities to Roman gods, and the prevalence of Greek philosophy among well-educated Romans, brought about an increasing neglect of the old rites, and in the 1st century BC, the

religious importance of the old priestly offices declined rapidly, though their civic importance and political influence remained. Roman religion in the empire tended more and more to centre on the imperial house, and several emperors were deified after their deaths. Under the empire, the Romans absorbed the mythologies of their conquered subjects, often leading to situations in which the temples and priests of traditional Italian deities existed side by side with those of foreign gods. Numerous foreign religions grew popular, such as the worship of the Egyptian Isis and the Persian Mithras. Beginning in the 2nd century, Christianity began to spread in the Empire, despite initial persecution. Beginning with Emperor Nero, Roman official policy towards Christianity was negative, and at some points, simply being a Christian could be punishable by death. Under Emperor Diocletian, the persecution of Christians reached its peak. However, it became an officially supported religion in the Roman state under Constantine I and became exponentially popular. After a brief and unsuccessful pagan revival by the emperor Julian the Apostate, Christianity became the permanent religion of the empire. All religions except Christianity were prohibited in 391 by an edict of Emperor Theodosius I.[2]

A vital part of each of these ancient kingdoms was the worship of their gods. These people depended on the help of their gods to win their battles. They believed the gods played an important role in the lives of mankind and of nations, and this belief still resides among people today in one form or the other. Mankind was created by God and embedded with a desire to earnestly worship through respect and homage. As we saw, in the ancient Roman Empire, the sacred king took on the religious responsibilities of the deposed kings, and the emperors were held to be gods. And in all these empires, emperors were treated much as gods were. We see an example of this when Mordecai refused to bow down to Haman: "When Haman saw that Mordecai did not bow or pay him homage, Haman was filled with wrath" (Esther 3:5).

Unlike those of old, who believed in the gods for victory in battle or for their way of life, the world today through its knowledge and technology believes in its own ability, power, and strength. People no longer believe like those of old in gods who will lead them in battle or in the way they should live. Yet, because of this self-confidence, people today fail to realize that they have become their own gods. Every human being has a god in his or her life. For you, that god could be yourself, because anything you worship is your god. People might say there is no God or they don't believe in any gods, but without even realizing it, they have built their own gods in their lives. Yet, the only true God still loves us all despite our misdirected worship and beliefs. The Bible says, "He makes His sun rise on the evil and on the good, and sends rain on the just and on the unjust" (Matthew 5:45).

Ask yourself this question: What am I living for? Your answer will enable you to see what you are worshipping as your god. It could be your family, your children, your job, wealth, or power and influence in your society. You might say to yourself, "But I do not see it as a god." Maybe you don't, but it has become a god for you. On the other hand, there are many who believe there is one God, as the Word of God teaches. Such belief is to be commended, but it is not enough, for even the demons believe there is one God. James wrote, "You believe that there is one God. You do well. Even the demons believe and tremble!" (James 2:19). You may believe there is one God, but do you worship the one and only God? Do you worship the Creator of the heavens and the earth, the God of Israel? Are you worshipping Him or worshipping His creation? The honest answer is what you confess with your mouth and believe in your heart.

We do not intend to change your mind on the issue of whether there is or isn't one God and whether you worship Him or not. We seek only to show you where you truly stand on these matters. And the key to knowing people—even ourselves—is what they do. The Bible says, "You will know them by their fruits" (Matthew 7:16).

Let us define the word *God*. What does this word mean? How much influence does God have in your life? Do you depend on God in making decisions? Or is God just a word that has no impact on your life?

God is "the one Supreme Being, the creator and ruler of the universe. God is the name of the Divine Being. It is the rendering of the Hebrew 'El, from a word meaning to be strong."[3] Does this definition fit you or those to whom you ascribe worship?

To explain the supremacy of the almighty God, let's look at the book of 1 Samuel, when Israel lost the Ark of the Covenant to the Philistines. The supremacy of God the Creator can be seen in how the presence of the Ark of the Covenant destroyed the Philistines' god, Dagon.

> Then the Philistines took the ark of God and brought it from Ebenezer to Ashdod. When the Philistines took the ark of God, they brought it into the house of Dagon and set it by Dagon. And when the people of Ashdod arose early in the morning, there was Dagon, fallen on its face to the Earth before the ark of the LORD. So they took Dagon and set it in its place again. And when they arose early the next morning, there was Dagon, fallen on its face to the ground before the ark of the LORD. The head of Dagon and both the palms of its hands were broken off on the threshold; only Dagon's torso was left of it. (1 Samuel 5:1–5)

Not only did the presence of the ark of the covenant of the God of Israel destroy the Philistine god, Dagon, but in whatever city the

Ark of the Covenant was kept, there was great destruction.

> So they carried the ark of the God of Israel away. So it was, after they had carried it away, that the hand of the LORD was against the city with a very great destruction; and He struck the men of the city, both small and great, and tumors broke out on them. (1 Samuel 5:8–9)

It is interesting to note that the ark of the covenant of the God of Israel destroyed the god of the Philistines, Dagon. The more they kept the Ark of the Covenant, the more calamities befell them. Were these acts by chance, or was it really the God of Israel at work? The Philistines wanted to know. So the Philistines sent the ark on its way, believing the condition they placed on it would explain the cause of the evil that befell them.

> "Watch: if it goes up the road to its own territory, to Beth Shemesh, then He has done us this great evil. But if not, then we shall know that it is not His hand that struck us—it happened to us by chance." (1 Samuel 6:9)

They didn't have to wait for long for their answer.

> Then the cows headed straight for the road to Beth Shemesh, and went along the highway, lowing as they went, and did not turn aside to the right hand or the left. And the lords of the Philistines went after them to the border of Beth Shemesh. (1 Samuel 6:12)

The cows carrying the Ark of the Covenant went straight on to Beth Shemesh, to the Israelites. This proved to the Philistines that the great evil that befell them was from the hand of the most supreme God. Can the god you worship do such great wonders and stand up for himself as the God of the Israelites did? Or do you have to fight for your god because he cannot fight for himself? What or who are you worshipping? Who is your God?

If you believe in the Creator of the heavens and the earth, the God of Israel, I sincerely wish you success; yet, as we know, there are many who claim no belief at all in God.

I am the father of three boys and three girls. One day the oldest boy brought one of his friends to visit at our home in Figtree, New South Wales, Australia. At home that day in the sitting room, I began to speak with this young lady, who was in her early twenties. One thing led to another, and I asked her whether she believed in God. She said no, she didn't believe in God. Her life was simply a matter of going to bed and waking up in the morning and going about her daily routine, and that was it. I knew before this that some people do not believe in God, but coming across this young lady and her confession of not believing in God raised some questions in my mind and caused me to appreciate more our Lord Jesus Christ and His salvation. Here are some of the questions that came to my mind: Is it possible not to believe in God? How could I live without God? Who am I? What do I believe in? Who or what is my god? What happens after death? I can tell you I felt scared. Even today when I think about that situation, I still feel fear.

Why be afraid? I really can't tell, but just the thought of not believing and knowing God is scary. As we discussed earlier, in the old days people believed in something, and they fought for what they believed in. There were—and still are—some who will even die for what they believe. Consider the biblical story of the three Hebrew boys Shadrach, Meshach, and Abed-Nego, who were reported to King Nebuchadnezzar for not worshipping the golden image the king set up. The king warned them to worship the image and told them of the consequences of disobeying his orders. "If you do not worship, you shall be cast immediately into the midst of a burning fiery furnace. And who is the god who will deliver you from my hands?" (Daniel 3:15).

I love the response of the Hebrew boys. Their faith in the almighty God is awesome.

> Shadrach, Meshach, and Abed-Nego answered and said to the king, "O Nebuchadnezzar, we have no need to answer you in this matter. If that is the case, our God whom we serve is able to deliver us from the burning fiery furnace, and He will deliver us from your hand, O king. But if not, let it be known to you, O king, that we do not serve your gods, nor will we worship the gold image which you have set up." (Daniel 3:16–18)

Shadrach, Meshach and Abed-Nego, young Hebrew boys, believed in the God of Israel and were willing to die for what they believed. They told King Nebuchadnezzar that the God they served was able to deliver them from the burning fiery furnace, and even if He did not deliver them, they still would not bow to the gold image the king had set up. What a belief! Because of this statement, the king became furious and was determined to know which of the gods was going to deliver them from the fiery furnace. If you read on in the Bible, you will see that the only Savior and Deliverer, the God of Israel, sent His Son, Jesus Christ, to set them free. Sometimes we are tested, and we lose the battle because our trust is lacking or is misplaced. If you ask me, I will boldly tell you that the God who created the heavens and the earth and made mankind and put him on the earth is able to protect us and deliver us from every fiery furnace of our lives. We can choose to be like the young lady I spoke about earlier, who has not discovered what she believes in, or we can try to discover what it is we truly believe in. The Bible says, "The fool has said in his heart, 'There is no God.' They are corrupt, they have done abominable works, there is none who does good" (Psalm 14:1). But "the Scripture says, 'Whoever believes on Him will not be put to shame'" (Romans 10:11). We have the truth to believe and the power to believe it. What do you believe in today?

In our time, what our world leaders have called the war on terrorism shows that there are people today, perhaps including you and me, who are willing to stand and even die for the values and principles they believe in. For example, consider those who take their own lives through suicide bombings. What goes on inside the mind of a suicide bomber?

> Suicide bombers are motivated by a "simple cost-benefit analysis," in which the 'benefits' of self-destruction outweigh the cost. The benefits are perceived by the terrorist to be so great—in terms of membership of the group, achievement of collective goals, the promise of benefits in the after-life, and so on—that they outweigh the cost. Suicide bombers are not mentally ill or unhinged, but acting rationally in pursuit of the 'benefits' they perceive from being part of a strict and close-knit religious enterprise. Research shows the widely-held view of suicide bombers as brain-washed religious fanatics, vulnerable through youth and poverty, is not an accurate one. While religion plays a central role—there are few instances of non-religiously motivated suicide attacks—the suicide bomber is also driven on another level by a rational thought process. This is the desire to be part of a group that engenders strength and solidarity from strictness, and encourages members to submit totally to the collective aims of the group. Being part of an exclusive group with very strict beliefs requires intense commitment, and engenders a deep belief in shared

experience and self-sacrifice. In this way there is a 'marriage' of violence and religion, via the suicide bombers' participation in the group. Suicide bombing is just an extension of this self-sacrifice—the ultimate extension. The benefits are perceived to be so great as to justify the action.[4]

Belief is a powerful tool we humans have. It can be used to build up and to break down, to scatter or to bring together, to make war or to make peace. The question is this: What are you using your belief for? Whatever our belief is, it will be associated with one of the existing orders operating over the earth. We can appreciate those who are studying human behavior, trying to rationalize the why behind behavior patterns. Though they refuse to accept the *order of darkness* and the *order of light* that exist over the earth and God's dominion over His creation, we can agree with them that there are always questions that need to be answered, questions that relate to a person's belief system.

Let us look at the account of the mysterious writing on the wall in the Bible.

> Then they brought the gold vessels that had been taken from the temple of the house of God which had been in Jerusalem; and the king and his lords, his wives, and his concubines drank from them. They drank wine, and praised the gods of gold and silver, bronze and iron, wood and stone. In the same hour the

fingers of a man's hand appeared and wrote opposite the lampstand on the plaster of the wall of the king's palace; and the king saw the part of the hand that wrote. (Daniel 5:3–5)

What is the importance of this passage of Scripture we just read? What has it to do with the power of belief? We see King Belshazzar, the successor of Nebuchadnezzar, celebrating with his statesmen and his wives, along with his concubines. After becoming drunk, they began to praise the gods of gold and silver, bronze and iron, wood, and stone. They believed those things were gods; therefore the God of those things had to make known to those present that those things were not gods but were *for* God the almighty, who made them. Therefore God, the creator of gold and silver, bronze and iron, wood and stone, said to Belshazzar the king, through an interpreter, the prophet Daniel, "This is the interpretation of each word. MENE: God has numbered your kingdom, and finished it; TEKEL: You have been weighed in the balances, and found wanting; PERES: Your kingdom has been divided, and given to the Medes and Persians" (Daniel 5: 26–28). This incident marked the end of King Belshazzar's life and reign. A similar end awaits all those who disregard the almighty God.

We live for what we believe. Whenever we stop believing, we stop living. Whenever we stop believing, we stop existing. When our belief system shuts down, we find it hard to live any longer. Some people even go to the extent of taking their own lives. It is said that "losers are quitters, and quitters are losers," but we say "not believing is not living, and not living is not believing." People who do not believe in God go to bed and believe within themselves that they will wake up in the morning and go about their activities; some have plans for a month, a year, or even years from now! They are not concerned about whether they will wake up or not because they believe they will, and they usually do. They do not believe in God, but they still believe in something.

As we discussed in chapter 1, different kinds of battles entangle our lives. We overcome these trials because what we believe motivates and energizes us to keep going. It is commendable that we believe in something. Why? Because there is always hope that we can channel that ability *to* believe toward the truth we *should* believe. Consider the man Cornelius in the Bible. Although he believed in God, he did not know the way to God. However, through his belief and dedicated heart, he was given direction to the true God by an angel of God in a vision. For a full version of the story, please read the whole of Acts 10. For now, we will share some sections of the chapter here.

> About the ninth hour of the day he saw clearly in a vision an angel of God coming in and saying to him, "Cornelius!" And when he observed him, he was afraid, and said, "What is it, lord?" So he said to him, "Your prayers and your alms have come up for a memorial before God. Now send men to Joppa, and send for Simon whose

surname is Peter. He is lodging with Simon, a tanner, whose house is by the sea. He will tell you what you must do." (Acts 10:3–6)

The instruction to Cornelius from the angel of God was direct and precise. Through a vision, God prepared Simon Peter to receive the men Cornelius sent to him. If you do not believe in God, this book is a "vision" for you to know Him.

While Peter thought about the vision, the Spirit said to him, "Behold, three men are seeking you. Arise therefore, go down and go with them, doubting nothing; for I have sent them." (Acts 10:19–20)

This is the God we serve. He is not a God of confusion. When we walk with Him, He will direct our paths and guide us in what to do. If you continue reading in the Bible, you will find that Cornelius, his family, and his friends received salvation, spoke in new tongues, and were water baptized. In seeking to know God, Cornelius found the true God not only for himself but also for his family and community. If we seek the true God, we will find Him.

If people want to find their Creator, they can. God is not hiding Himself from us; He has already made Himself known to us through His creation. This is what King Solomon, the wisest king said: "That which has been is what will be, that which is done is what will be done, and there is nothing new under the sun" (Ecclesiastes 1:9). We should not reinvent the wheel. If our great-grandfathers founded and established the great inheritance we possess and live in today and then passed it on to us, then we need to know where their strength came from. It may or may not be necessary for us to follow their example, but history tells us we build on the legacy of our forefathers. As we build on a legacy of faith in God, we experience improved life over the years.

Many live with doubt about the existence of God. Why? I could attempt to answer by saying it is because people have felt the God of the church has let them down or God did not show up when they called on Him. But what people fail to recognize is who their god really is or what their god really is. How easy is it to shift blame for our own failures onto God. Some people in the past did this, blaming God for what befell them. Here is God's response to them through His prophet Ezekiel.

> "Yet you say, 'The way of the Lord is not fair.' Hear now, O house of Israel, is it not My way which is fair, and your ways which are not fair? When a righteous man turns away from his righteousness, commits iniquity, and dies in it, it is because of the iniquity which he has done that he dies. Again, when a wicked man turns away from the wickedness which he committed, and does what is lawful and right, he preserves himself alive. Because he considers and turns away from all the transgressions which he committed, he shall surely live; he shall not die." (Ezekiel 18:25-28)

God's command was plain to the house of Israel. If we sin and die without repenting, we have no eternal life with God. On the other hand, if we die with a repentant heart and faith in Jesus Christ, we have eternal life with God Almighty. So missing out on eternal life with God cannot be blamed on God but only on us for not choosing God.

Our failure to acknowledge our separation from God has kept us from awakening to the deceit of the dark order. The house of Israel believed they could play the harlot and go scot-free. They thought merely being children of Abraham gave them a righteousness that was eternal, and it did not matter what they did, whether they worshiped other gods or not. They believed they were still the people of God. So it is with the church today. Some Christians today believe that once saved is forever saved. I have news for you. If you do not turn from your sin, even though you have accepted Jesus Christ as your Lord and Savior, you will be rejected by our Lord Jesus Christ. That is why God put it so clearly. If you are a sinner and you repent and turn from your wicked ways and do what is lawful, you will preserve your life. And if you turn away from your righteousness and commit iniquity and die in your iniquity, it is because of your iniquity you have died.

2.1 The Fall of Mankind

All have sinned and fall short of the glory of God. (Romans 3:23)

After receiving our Lord Jesus Christ into my life, I desired with expectation an adventure with Him. One day I was listening to one of my favorite preachers from the United State of America, and the preacher said, "THE KINGDOM OF GOD IS NOT ABOUT *DOS AND DON'TS.*" Another time, as I was talking with some friends, we began to discuss Christianity and the church. One of them said the church is full of dos and don'ts. It took a while, but I felt the Spirit of God leading me to actually sit and meditate on this issue of dos and don'ts. I then realized that from childhood dos and don'ts are a way of governance within the family, the community, and even the world. Every family today governs with dos and don'ts. Why? Is it because parents want their children to be their puppets? Perhaps that is true in some cases, but there is a biblical reason for parents to employ a system of dos and don'ts. Paul wrote, "Children, obey your parents in the Lord, for this is right. 'Honor your father and mother,' which is the first commandment with promise: 'that it may be well with you and you may live long on the Earth'" (Ephesians 6:1–3). It is the parents' responsibility to help their children grow to obey the dos and don'ts of life.

Every sovereign nation in our world today governs with dos and don'ts. Is this because they want to control the masses and have them bent to the rule of law? Perhaps this is what motivates some, but, again, there is a biblical reason for governing this way. Paul wrote this:

> Let every soul be subject to the governing authorities. For there is no authority

except from God, and the authorities that exist are appointed by God. Therefore whoever resists the authority resists the ordinance of God and those who resist will bring judgment on themselves. For rulers are not terrors to good works, but to evil. Do you want to be unafraid of the authority? Do what is good, and you will have praise from the same. (Romans 13:1–3)

    The Bible commands us to respect our parents and the governing authorities of our nations. How do we do this? Isn't it done by the *dos-and-don'ts order* and rule? Imagine being employed by a company or an institution, where the *order of dos and don'ts* is not in place. Wouldn't that be cool? You would be able to go to work at any time or even stay home and still get paid!
    But imagine a world without the *dos-and-don'ts order*. With all the chaos and evil in the world today, where the *order of dos and don'ts* exists, what do you think would be happening if this order were not in place? Do you think this world would be a place we would want to live and raise a family? I think you will agree with me the answer is no. This *order of dos and don'ts* enables us to know the level and limits of our freedom; it motivates our potential and helps us become effective and efficient in our operations. Mankind was made with this instinct. Our five senses tell us what to do and what not to do and whether something is the right thing to do or not. We are governed by this *dos-and-don'ts*

order. In the absence of the dos and don'ts, people will do what is right in their own eyes. As recorded in the book of Judges, the people of Israel had been given laws, and the *order of dos and don'ts* were in place. However, in the absence of a leader or a king, the people did what was right in their own eyes (Judges 21:25). What a mess it was! Everyone doing his or her own thing may sound cool, but it was a mess. Because of this mess, God had to bring up a prophet to put the house of Israel in order.

There are some who feel they have to do what seems right in their eyes. Consequently, they find themselves in trouble with the authorities; many of them end up in prison. If there is a law, that means there are dos and don'ts. If you obey the law, you will save yourself much trouble. The world cannot exist without the *dos-*and*-don'ts order*. This is why we have laws to govern us; they make sure everyone does not do what seems right in his or her own eyes, resulting in utter chaos.

After considering all these matters, a question came to my mind: Why should God and the kingdom of God on the earth be any different? If you agree with me that the *order of dos and don'ts* exists for the good of a nation and her people, then you will agree with me that the *order of dos and don'ts* is also good for the kingdom of God and the church of God today.

I remember one day leaving the Illawarra TAFE College in North Wollongong in New South Wales, Australia, on my way to the University of Wollongong. My mobile phone rang and I decided to stop in a no-stopping zone for just one minute to answer it. I thought this was the right thing to do rather than try to answer the phone while I was driving, but it was wrong according to the law. Later I received a fine of two hundred and fifty dollars! Can you believe it? Yes, I paid two hundred and fifty dollars for a one-minute stop! The law did not ask me why I stopped there. It was not concerned about my safety. The law was not concerned about me but was concerned that the law had been broken. And the perpetrator had to be punished according to the law.

What the Lord taught me through this incident was this: If people can really mean what they say, as evidenced by their laws, doesn't God mean what He says? I was impressed with the straightforward nature of the *dos-and-don'ts order* in this case. At the same time, I learned never to stop in a no-stopping zone. Even though we may not agree with the dos or the don'ts at times, we still must follow them because they are the order of our time. The dos and don'ts rule over us and maintain order in society. Because of this order we are proud of our nation. We remain free citizens as long as we walk according to this *dos-and-don'ts order* of the law. However, we may become bound citizens if we disobey.

God does not find pleasure in any of us disobeying the law. Hear what He says: "'Do I have any pleasure at all that the wicked should die?' says the Lord God, 'and not that he should turn from his ways and live?'" (Ezekiel 18:23). No free nation wants to punish its citizens and see them suffer in prison, but lawbreakers must be punished—not only to protect others but also to help them learn to do what is right and to fit into society. So it is with God. Do we believe God takes pleasure in seeing the suffering we are going through under the *order of darkness* and its coworkers? It bleeds the heart of Jesus Christ. His hope is that we will decide to turn to Him and not be controlled by the *order of darkness* but by the *order of light*.

When God created man and gave mankind dominion over His creation, God also applied the *order of dos and don'ts*. He said to the first man, "Of the tree of the knowledge of good and evil you shall not eat, for in the day that you eat of it you shall surely die" (Genesis 2:17). Mankind was given the opportunity to enjoy this earth by simply obeying the order. This, of course, raises a question in our minds: Why did God leave the Tree of the Knowledge of Good and Evil in the garden? Or perhaps we could ask why God did not protect mankind from the tree. Was it His plan for mankind to fall? Is God good? Does He really love mankind?

Let's go back to the discussion on the existing *powers over earth* in which we learned the *order of darkness* and the *order of light* existed before God created or called forth the earth we live on.

> The earth [universe] was without form, and void; and darkness was on the face of the deep. And the Spirit of God was hovering over the face of the waters. Then God said, "Let there be light"; and there was light. ... Then God said, "Let the waters under the heavens be gathered

together into one place, and let the dry land appear"; and it was so. And God called the dry land Earth, and the gathering together of the waters He called Seas. And God saw that it was good. (Genesis 1:2-3, 9-10)

This third order (dos and don'ts) had to be put into place because Lucifer and his demons had established the *order of darkness* and God had to put in place the *order of light* to counteract and overcome the *order of darkness*. Therefore, mankind had to choose which order to obey, as we see in the case of Eve. Eve was confronted by the cunning serpent, who twisted the command of God. "Now the serpent was more cunning than any beast of the field which the LORD God had made. And he said to the woman, 'Has God indeed said, "You shall not eat of every tree of the garden"?'" (Genesis 3:1). Eve responded, saying, "We may eat the fruit of the trees of the garden; but of the fruit of the tree which is in the midst of the garden, God has said, 'You shall not eat it, nor shall you touch it, lest you die'" (verses 2-3). Then the serpent responded, "You will not surely die. For God knows that in the day you eat of it your eyes will be opened, and you will be like God, knowing good and evil" (verses 4-5). Look at what happened to Eve next: "So when the woman saw that the tree was good for food, that it was pleasant to the eyes, and a tree desirable to make one wise, she took of its fruit and ate. She also gave to her husband with her, and he ate" (verse 6).

This is the familiar account of the fall of man. It originated from the conversation between the serpent and Eve in the Garden of Eden. In Genesis 2:16, God told Adam he could freely eat of every tree of the garden. In Genesis 3:1, the serpent questioned God's word. This question was the first step in deceiving Eve. We should be very careful anytime someone questions what God's Word says because within that question is well-packaged deception, which we may not recognize until it is too late.

It is interesting to note that Adam and Eve may have been in the garden for several years (only God knows how long), and they must have passed by this Tree of the Knowledge of Good and Evil and even taken shade under it. To them, it must have seemed like any other tree in the garden. But after the serpent questioned Eve, notice what occurred to her in verse 6. Suddenly, Eve saw the tree was good for food, pleasant to the eyes, and desirable to make one wise. For a moment, let's think about what happened, what occurred to Eve. The power of knowledge was perceived and desired.

Let us look around us today. Knowledge has empowered us to invent many helpful things, but the power of knowledge also brings into play the power of control and the power of lordship and injustice. An African proverb says the one-eyed man is the chief in the town of the blind. Knowledge has brought about slavery. People desire knowledge more than life, and so most people have become slaves to knowledge. This enslaving knowledge comes from disobedience, and it is corrupt. Therefore, it needs to be refined, and this is where God comes in. Without the refining work of God, we are pulled into knowledge that is deceiving, which is after the *order of darkness*. Specifically, this deception tells us all we see is gold, but in reality all that glitters is not gold.

Even before Eve ate of the fruit, she had sinned because of her desire. As James wrote,

> Let no one say when he is tempted, "I am tempted by God"; for God cannot be tempted by evil, nor does He Himself tempt anyone. But each one is tempted when he is drawn away by his own desires and enticed. Then, when desire has conceived, it gives birth to sin; and sin, when it is full-grown, brings forth death. (James 1:13–15)

We can see in Eve's fall that one part of the body has been pointed out: the eye. The Bible tells us our eyes can bring either light or darkness to our bodies.

> The lamp of the body is the eye. If therefore your eye is good, your whole body will be full of light. But if your eye is bad, your whole body will be full of darkness. If therefore the light that is in you is darkness, how great is that darkness! (Matthew 6:22–23)

The eye is a vital part of the body, for it is the light of the body. Eve had seen this tree;

now suddenly she saw that the fruit was desirable and pleasant to the eyes.

Over the years I have found myself going through this experience. I sometimes enter a shopping center and something in one of the stores catches my eye. Seemingly, I cannot resist it, and I find myself buying the item for myself. After a while I look at what I bought, and I say to myself, "Why did I buy this?" Perhaps you can identify with this experience. At one time or another, we all have found ourselves desiring something that captivates our eyes, and we cannot let go. So it was with Eve at that time; she could not let go of the tree.

But what causes this to happen? The answer is lust. As mentioned earlier in section 1.1.5, lust is a spiritual issue. It is a desire within us or before our eyes, whether for a person or a thing, and it is often sustained for a long time. Lust is a sin, and Jesus warned us, "But I say to you that whoever looks at a woman to lust for her has already committed adultery with her in his heart" (Matthew 5: 28). Recall the illustration we presented in chapter 1 from 2 Samuel 13:1–16. There we are told that Amnon lusted for his sister Tamar, but after having sex with her, he despised her greatly. Many people confuse lust with love. Amnon lusted for his sister Tamar to the extent that he grew thin! This is how powerful lust can be! When asked by a friend what the matter was, Amnon said to him, "I love Tamar, my brother Absalom's sister" (2 Samuel 13:4).

So, with the help of the friend, Amnon devised a plan. He pretended to be sick and asked his father, King David, to be served food by his sister Tamar. But "when she had brought them to him to eat, he took hold of her and said to her, 'Come, lie with me, my sister'" (2 Samuel 13:11).

Tamar pleaded with him but to no effect; the power of lust was too great. "He would not heed her voice; and being stronger than she, he forced her and lay with her" (2 Samuel 13:14). But did Amnon really love Tamar? Was it love or lust? He thought he loved her but soon realized he did not.

> Then Amnon hated her exceedingly, so that the hatred with which he hated her was greater than the love with which he had loved her. And Amnon said to her, "Arise, be gone!" So she said to him, "No, indeed! This evil of sending me away is worse than the other that you did to me." But he would not listen to her. (2 Samuel 13:15–16)

Consider what we just read in the Scriptures. Does this sound familiar in our world today? Lust is a powerful force or spirit that can control our lives if we permit it to. It will make use of every opportunity.

Lust can become obsessive. If you find yourself wanting something and being willing to go to almost any extent and use almost any means to get it, this is a manifestation of the spirit of lust. When you find yourself being controlled by the spirit of lust, experiencing an urgency to get someone or something in your life even at risk of losing your loved ones or your integrity, you need to seek help immediately. Most of us have seen the devastation caused by the spirit of lust in loved ones, families, and even nations. Whenever the eye lusts or we allow the spirit of lust to formulate our decisions, there will always be consequences.

    Let us see what happened to Adam and Eve when they ate the fruit.

> Then the eyes of both of them were opened, and they knew that they were naked; and they sewed fig leaves together and made themselves coverings. And they heard the sound of the LORD God walking in the garden in the cool of the day, and Adam and his wife hid themselves from the presence of the LORD God among the trees of the garden. (Genesis 3:7–8)

    Although the Bible uses the word *naked*, I will use the word *shame*. When one is shamed, he or she becomes vexed. Think of it. When you lusted after something and made the wrong decisions, you became ashamed of yourself and even angry.

    Many times, like Eve and Adam, we become puffed up with pride. We refuse to humble ourselves and express our sorrow. Instead, we walk away in pride like Adam and Eve. Like them, we run away and hide ourselves from God, too proud to tell the Lord we are sorry for what we have done. Sadly, we sink down in our pride and shame! How many of us even say we are sorry to the authorities when we are caught in a wrong? We try to justify our actions, even though we know within ourselves we are guilty. How pathetic are our actions! We need help. Adam and Eve were fortunate and received God's help. What about you? Are you running from Him or reaching out for Him?

2.2   God's Reaction and Provision

> The wages of sin is death, but the gift of God is eternal life in Christ Jesus our Lord. (Romans 6:23)

For every action, there is a reaction. In 2009 I was asked by one of the sisters at our church to assist her with transportation so she could go look at a home that was available to rent. That morning I dropped my son off at school and left for the sister's house to pick her up. The lady got into the car, and we started down a little hill. Within fifty meters, I tried to apply the brakes because we were approaching a curve, but the brakes did not work! By the grace of God, we drove into a tree without further damage to lives or homes. I began to wonder what went wrong and why the brakes had suddenly failed!

As I sat in my wondering world, a fire truck arrived with the emergency lights on, followed by an ambulance and the police. It was overwhelming to see this level of concern for the safety of people. To God be the glory, we were all fine. I had to give a report to the police regarding the incident. I told them the brakes of the vehicle had failed, but the car had just been serviced within the past four months. After the incident report, the car was towed away. Only then did a little relief come to me. We walked back to the sister's house and thanked the Lord it had not been worse. His grace covered us, and we were safe.

About four or five months after the accident, I received a fine of over three hundred dollars from the police for driving a defective vehicle. What the police were saying was that I had to be punished for the action. The report I gave about the service of the car did not matter. Because there was an action—the accident—the reaction from the police was a fine. Although I did not like the police's decision to fine me, I learned from the incident the rationale for the fine, which I believe was the safety of lives and property. I also learned I was responsible for my actions.

The world we live in today stands ready to react to the actions of those who want to disregard the dos and don'ts of society. Many times our actions, whether positive or negative, are driven by an inner gut passion that compels us to act without taking into account the consequences. What else could possibly drive someone to walk into a supermarket and suddenly start shooting other customers indiscriminately? To gain an idea of what goes on in such a situation and how people are affected, let us look at some of the recent massacres in American schools.

> On Friday December 14, 2012, twenty children were massacred at a Connecticut

elementary school in the USA. "Every single person who is watching the news today is asking 'Where is God when this happens?'" says Max Lucado, a prominent Christian pastor based in San Antonio. In all, 28 people died, including 26 victims at the school and the gunman himself, widely reported to be 20-year-old Adam Lanza, a loner who some said suffered from a personality disorder and possibly Asperger's Syndrome. The final victim appeared to be the mother of the shooter, Nancy Lanza, whose body was later found at the home they shared. Investigators had put together a grim timeline of cruel butchery. After allegedly robbing his mother of her life, the shooter seemingly drove in her car to the Sandy Hook Elementary in Newtown, which lies some 65 miles northeast from New York City. At around 9.30 am he burst into a kindergarten class and unleashed a deliberate and unremitting fusillade of bullets. He was armed with two automatic pistols. A semi-automatic rifle was later found in the car he had left inside. Some reports said the firearms had been registered to Nancy Lanza. The Governor of Connecticut, Dannel Malloy, was direct. "Evil visited this community today," he said.

The shooting is the latest such incident to hit America, with the number dead reported to be more than double those killed at Columbine High School in Colorado, where 13 people were killed in the infamous massacre in 1999. More recently, shootings have occurred in Colorado, which was hit by an attack at a midnight showing of the new Batman film, and a Sikh temple in Wisconsin. At Virginia Tech, a university, 32 people were left dead following a massacre by a student in 2007. On each occasion, there have been ritual rumblings about the need for greater gun control, but little meaningful action. Referring to the litany of tragedies, the President yesterday called for another effort in that direction. "As a country, we have been through this too many times ... We're going to have to come together and take meaningful action to prevent more tragedies like this, regardless of the politics," he said.[5]

In the midst of such heinous actions, the reaction of the police is to protect and save lives and try to apprehend or take down the perpetrators carrying out the violence. After the perpetrators are apprehended, certain rights are afforded them. They get a lawyer or are given a lawyer to assist them with their case. They can plead guilty or not guilty, seek to confirm insanity, or pursue whatever avenue that might give them a good case. We live in a world that has provided a response plan for perpetrators of crime.

As these incidents unfolded in the USA, we heard people asking the question, "Where is

God?" Others declared that evil had visited the community. How many of us really want to know where God is, or do we just want to play the blame game? We trust our government and the law we have in place to bring perpetrators to justice and to protect us. In the same way, God has made laws for mankind to live by—even though some say God's ways are not fair (see Ezekiel 18:26–29). Why do we blame God for what happens to us or our loved ones, when we are not under His protection, guidance, and instructions? Why blame God or even ask where He is in time of crisis, when in reality we do not want to know where He is? When God created mankind in the beginning, He used to come in the cool of the day to visit and, I believe, to talk with Adam and Eve. But when they sinned, they hid themselves from God: "Adam and his wife hid themselves from the presence of the Lord God among the trees of the garden" (Genesis 3:8).

Growing up with a single mother, I always appreciated seeing my mother coming home from work in the evening because she made me feel safe. Our relationship with our heavenly Father should be even better. Jesus said, "If you then, being evil, know how to give good gifts to your children, how much more will your Father who is in heaven give good things to those who ask Him!" (Matthew 7:11). If only we knew what we were missing!

During the tribal wars in Liberia, people were being killed based simply on their tribe—who they were. During this time, a friend and sister in the Lord shared her testimony with us. She said one day the soldiers came to her home on Bushrod Island in Logan Town in Liberia. At that time she and her husband had gone home to find some food to take to their children, who had taken refuge two to three kilometers away from the house. When the soldiers came, her husband escaped and left her alone. The soldiers began to use profane words. One of them said to the others, "Let's kill her." He pointed his gun at her and fired several shots. Because of fear, she dropped as if dead. They thought she was actually dead, and they left. Later on—I believe quickened by the Holy Spirit—she got up and began to feel her body and said to herself, "I'm not dead!" She thanked the Lord for His protection over her life.

If only we can turn back to God, who is willing and ready to receive us, we will experience safety that no man can give. The apostle Peter said, "The Lord is not slack concerning His promise, as some count slackness, but is longsuffering toward us, not willing that any should perish but that all should come to repentance" (2 Peter 3:9). Instead of playing god and then, when we are destroyed by the *order of darkness*, wondering where God is, let us go back to Him, for He is willing to receive us. As 2 Chronicles 7:14 says, "If My people who are called by My name will humble themselves, and pray and seek My face, and turn from their wicked ways, then I will hear from heaven, and will forgive their sin and heal their land." This is a guarantee, and it is the only way we can be safe. We need to search for and return to the *order of light,* which will eliminate the *order of darkness*. If we don't, we will always ask, "Where is God?"

or simply say evil has visited our community. We will not receive much help. I can assure you the massacres recounted above were not the first and will not be the last such incidents to occur. Those wanting God's protection need to be under the *order of light*; then they will be protected, just as this sister was protected from the Evil One. As Christians, we believe that even if those who are under the *order of light* sleep and are no longer alive in the physical realm, they are living with the God of light.

    God created us, and He knows we need security. We like to feel safe and to be safe, and God provided this security by coming in the cool of the day to Adam and Eve. But by disobeying their heavenly Father's order not to eat of the fruit of the Tree of the Knowledge of Good and Evil, Adam and Eve became ashamed and saw that they were naked. Their first reaction was to try to fix what they had done. "They sewed fig leaves together and made themselves coverings" (Genesis 3:7).

    Adam and Eve tried to fix the problem by covering themselves. It appears we have an inborn tendency to try to fix things when we or someone else has spoiled them. Let us look at the case of King David. After he had made Uriah's wife pregnant, he tried to "fix" it. Sadly, this resulted in murder. King David recalled Uriah from the battlefield with the hope that Uriah would sleep with his wife and the unborn child would naturally be thought to be Uriah's child. However, his plan did not succeed. "Uriah slept at the door of the king's house with all the servants of his lord, and did not go down to his house" (2 Samuel 11:9).

David tried again, but his plan failed a second time. Then under the influence of the *order of darkness,* David devised a "better" plan. This he was sure would succeed. What was this "better" plan? It was murder. Let's read on.

> In the morning it happened that David wrote a letter to Joab and sent it by the hand of Uriah. And he wrote in the letter, saying, "Set Uriah in the forefront of the hottest battle, and retreat from him, that he may be struck down and die." So it was, while Joab besieged the city, that he assigned Uriah to a place where he knew there were valiant men. Then the men of the city came out and fought with Joab. And some of the people of the servants of David fell; and Uriah the Hittite died also. (2 Samuel 11:14–17)

David messed up, and he tried to fix it. How sad what the *order of darkness* can lead us to do when we allow it. Because he wanted to cover his shame, he became a murderer. Whenever we try to fix some wrong we have done, we always make it worse. There are some things within our power to fix, but there are some things beyond our power to fix, as in the case of Adam and Eve. Being naïve, they believed the fig leaves could cover their shame and nakedness. Massacres like the ones we talked about earlier are beyond the power of man to prevent. Gun control is not the answer.

Getting rid of the *order of darkness* in and over our lives and our nations is the answer. It is only the *order of light* that can make the difference, and the source of the *order of light* is God. The *order of light* is Jesus Christ. To cover our shame, we come up with more regulations that may seem good, but they result only in more control by man, not God.

After the disobedience of mankind, God in His infinite mercy responded by asking Adam where he was.

> Then the LORD God called to Adam and said to him, "Where are you?" So he said, "I heard Your voice in the garden, and I was afraid because I was naked; and I hid myself." And He said, "Who told you that you were naked? Have you eaten from the tree of which I commanded you that you should not eat?" Then the man said, "The woman whom You gave to be with me, she gave me of the tree, and I ate." And the LORD God said to the woman, "What is this you have done?" The woman said, "The serpent deceived me, and I ate." (Genesis 3:9–13)

We can see the love and the disappointment of God the Father when He asked Adam, "Where are you?" and "Who told you that you were naked?" God knew they were naked, but He was very disappointed and, I believe, sorry for the consequences that had to come into play. Like many today, Adam and Eve played the blame game instead of owning up to their actions and repenting. Adam blamed Eve, and Eve blamed the serpent. Whenever we disobey our parents, they become disappointed in us. They try to explain to us our mistake so we can confess our sin and be reconciled to them. But even with forgiveness, our parents must discipline us by grounding us or administering what suits the occasion. So it is with our Creator as we read from the book of Genesis. There were consequences to disobeying God. The serpent, the woman, and Adam each had to pay for their actions. What were the consequences to the serpent?

> So the LORD God said to the serpent: "Because you have done this, you are cursed more than all cattle, and more than every beast of the field; on your belly you shall go, and you shall eat dust all the days of your life. And I will put enmity between you and the woman, and between your seed and her Seed; he shall bruise your head, and you shall bruise His heel." (Genesis 3:14–15)

How about the consequences to the woman?

> To the woman He said: "I will greatly multiply your sorrow and your conception; in pain you shall bring forth children; your desire shall be for your husband, and he shall rule over you." (Genesis 3:16)

What about the consequences to Adam?

> Then to Adam He said, "Because you have heeded the voice of your wife, and have eaten from the tree of which I commanded

you, saying, 'You shall not eat of it':
"Cursed is the ground for your sake; in toil
you shall eat of it all the days of your life.
Both thorns and thistles it shall bring forth
for you, and you shall eat the herb of the
field. In the sweat of your face you shall
eat bread till you return to the ground, for
out of it you were taken; for dust you are,
and to dust you shall return." (Genesis
3:17–19)

After God set forth the consequences of Adam and Eve's disobedience, He made a provision for them. "Also for Adam and his wife the LORD God made tunics of skin, and clothed them" (Genesis 3:21).

When God told Adam the day he ate of the fruit of the Tree of the Knowledge of Good and Evil he would surely die, God meant it. Adam and Eve's disobedience brought into motion spiritual, physical, and eternal death. We see in God's pronouncements two kinds of death taking place in the life of mankind at the beginning. The first is spiritual: "Of the tree of the knowledge of good and evil you shall not eat, for in the day that you eat of it you shall surely die" (Genesis 2:17). The second is physical: "In the sweat of your face you shall eat bread till you return to the ground, for out of it you were taken; for dust you are, and to dust you shall return" (Genesis 3:19).

This is how spiritual and physical death came into play after Adam and Eve disobeyed God and before they were sent out of the Garden of Eden. Because they ate of the fruit of the Tree of the Knowledge of Good and Evil, they were sent out of the garden of God, signifying their spiritual death. Banishment from the garden also assured their eventual physical death.

Therefore the LORD God sent him out of the Garden of Eden to till the ground from which he was taken. So He drove out the man; and He placed cherubim at the east of the garden of Eden, and a flaming sword which turned every way, to guard the way to the tree of life (Genesis 3:23–24).

The Lord God sent them out of the Garden of Eden, the garden of God. Since then, mankind has been going and is still going far away from the presence of God.

How many of us want to receive instructions and directions for the betterment of our life? Young people today refuse to receive wisdom, but King Solomon in his wisdom said, "My son, hear the instruction of your father, and do not forsake the law of your mother" (Proverbs 1:8). We see a generation growing up without the knowledge and the wisdom of God. What a predicament! When God made mankind, He put mankind in His presence. Mankind's choice to disobey God was also a choice to be out of God's presence; so it is now people's responsibility to find God and apologize for their actions.

You might say, "I wasn't the one who did the act." You are right, but you are carrying on the act. Because we are continuing Adam and Eve's disobedience, we need to return to God and ask Him to forgive us for all of our disobedience. If we are not proud and choose to humble ourselves before God and ask for His forgiveness, He will forgive us and save us from the *order of darkness* as we walk according to His Word. As we discussed in chapter 1, we can now say that man found himself existing under three orders: the *order of darkness,* the *order of light,* and the *order of dos and don'ts.* But do the *order of light* and the *order of darkness* really influence mankind on the earth? We will be looking at this question in section 2.3.

Understanding the *order of light* and the *order of darkness* will help us understand ourselves. Whether or not we believe these orders exist does not erase their existence. We still find ourselves exercising and manifesting the fruits of these orders. For example, we cannot deny that our world today experiences a level of peace because of the *order of dos and don'ts.*

2.3 Life Outside of Eden

> Do not be deceived, God is not mocked; for whatever a man sows, that he will also reap. (Galatians 6:7)

I grew up with my brothers and sisters in a three-bedroom house. When I became a youth, I thought I knew it all and was on top of the world. I became a strong-willed and stiff-necked person. In the eyes of my understanding, I believed what I was doing was right. But in the eyes of my mother, who was both dad and mom to me, I was a pain and a troubled son. My mom decided to put me out of the house at age eighteen or nineteen and sent me to live with my dad. Without a repentant heart, I felt it was cool to change locations. But you never appreciate your surroundings, family, and friends until you lose them or separate from them.

I moved over to my dad's, and for the first week I felt good and thought it was going to work. I didn't think I needed to go back to live with my mom, my brothers, and my sisters, who lived between two and three kilometers away within walking distance from me. After the first week, though, I began to feel lonely and bored. Within a month I told my dad I had to go back to live with my mom. I could no longer bear being away from my dwelling place, my brothers and sisters, and the place where I grew up. My dad took me back to my mom's house and said to me, "You will have to apologize to your mom," which was not an issue for me. I had to go back home. Oh what a feeling it was to be back there! Dad and I saw Mom when she came back that evening from work. I apologized for my misbehavior, and she accepted me back into the home.

When I think back, I believe the decision to go back and live with my mother was one of the best decisions I ever made. It was not that my dad was a bad man or provided a bad environment at his house. I just realized what a blessing and opportunity I had at my mom's to grow up with a family and not be alone. That experience also taught me to humble myself and apologize to people whenever I have done wrong or offended someone.

Life is a journey. When people are going on a journey, they set the date of departure and arrange transportation. They know the destination and when they plan to return. All this planning is done through the eyes of their understanding. But life is given and taken away by God, and the weird part is we don't know when life will be taken away from us. This is why Jesus said, "Do not fear those who kill the body but cannot kill the soul. But rather fear Him who is able to destroy both soul and body in hell" (Matthew 10:28).

One thing that has caught my attention is the care needed to avoid plagiarism. In writing this book, if we use another person's information, we have to give that person credit and the recognition. The question is, why don't we acknowledge the source of life—God? Instead, we parade ourselves as the source of this life. In discussing the battle of wealth in section 1.1.3, we read of a rich man who looked to himself as the source of his riches without knowing that his wealth belonged to God. We would do well to learn from this parable of Jesus in Luke 12:13–21. This life we have belongs to God, and we need to believe and remember that.

Over the years we have seen politicians, heads of governments and institutions, and CEOs, as well as average families and individuals around the world, plan their lives and their futures without even taking into account the source of life. They fail to consider in their plans the One who has given them this life and allows them to wake up in the morning and carry out their routines. They fail to recognize God in their plans. James gives us good advice about involving God in our plans: "Instead you ought to say, 'If the Lord wills, we shall live and do this or that'" (James 4:15).

We love to give honor to whomever honor is due. Therefore, it is time for us to start giving honor to God. As the source of life, He is due such honor. Our failure to honor Him essentially makes us guilty of plagiarism. This is why Paul directed the men of Athens to give honor to the true God. He said, "Men of Athens, I perceive that in all things you are very religious; for as I was passing through and considering the objects of your worship, I even found an altar with this inscription: 'TO THE UNKNOWN GOD.' Therefore, the One whom you worship without knowing, Him I proclaim to you" (Acts 17:22–23). If those of old respected that which they did not know, we should certainly honor the God we know as the Giver of life.

As we said, life is a journey, and this journey is full of surprises—some good and some bad. If you look back and take inventory of your life's journey, you will be amazed. Perhaps your persistence and motivation brought you this far, and that is commendable. Not all will have a happy story of success, but not all will have a sad story of failure either. Whatever your story is, let me ask you this: Have you thanked the source of life for the life you now live, whether it is good or bad? You might argue, "What did He do that is worthy of my thanks?" Allow me to ask you another question: Are you still alive? If you are reading this book, then your answer is yes. That is why you should thank God: He is the source of your life.

Over the years while in Australia, I have come across people who say, "I used to thank God for my life, but I do not see any reason why I should do so anymore. We now have the answer to everything in life through science and technology." What is the rationale for acknowledging the source of life? It is plagiarism if we fail to acknowledge the sources of any material we use. It is also plagiarism if we fail to acknowledge God as the Giver of life, and we stand guilty of a sin that can result in God rejecting us. Indeed, in the past God has rejected those who failed to acknowledge Him. See what the apostle Paul said in Romans 1:28: "And even as they did not like to retain God in their knowledge, God gave them over to a debased mind, to do those things which are not fitting."

Have you ever thought about what could happen in the next minute? Our failure to acknowledge the one and only almighty God, who is the source of life, has left us with a world full of evil, controlled by the *order of darkness*. If you wonder why things are happening the way they are, this is a part of the answer: Mankind has been given up to his own lust. When there are calamities, we want to ask where God is in all of these. We are living according to our lust, and we are committed to this path that is leading us to destruction. And we want to know where God is? We know the answer. God is nowhere around because we have told Him He is not welcome. He is not welcome in our family, in our church, in our community, and even in our nation. By the way, God respects our decision, and He is staying out. We have the power to change all that is happening in our lives, our families, our churches, our communities, and even our nation, if we are willing to come together and turn to God, the source of life, and begin to live this new life that comes through Jesus Christ His Son.

We have seen God's reaction to man's disobeying the *dos-and-don'ts order*: He sent mankind out from His presence (Genesis 3:22–24). When man was created, he found himself in the light that was in the Garden of Eden, the garden of God. Leaving the garden of God brought a new experience for mankind, just as my leaving the place where I grew up was a new beginning for me. For mankind, however, it meant moving from blessings to curses. "Cursed is the ground for your sake; in toil you shall eat of it all the days of your life" (Genesis 3:17), the Lord said.

As the number of people increased on the face of the earth, it seems they began to undergo changes inwardly that were manifested outwardly; thus anger resulted in the first murder on the earth, despite the Lord's gracious intervention.

> So the LORD said to Cain, "Why are you angry? And why has your countenance fallen? If you do well, will you not be accepted? And if you do not do well, sin lies at the door. And its desire is for you, but you should rule over it." (Genesis 4:6–7)

But Cain did not heed the Lord's wise advice.

> Now Cain talked with Abel his brother; and it came to pass, when they were in the field, that Cain rose up against Abel his brother and killed him. (Genesis 4:8)

We talk about the massacres in American schools, and each day we listen to the news and hear that someone has killed someone else. In the case of Cain, God gave him the opportunity to reconsider his angry thoughts. But because of the dark order that controlled him, he was unwilling to rethink his decision. Therefore, he carried out his plan. As we said, to every action there is a reaction. If you read on in the Bible, you will see that Cain was punished by God for his action. The question that comes to mind, however, is this: If Abel was righteous and his offering was accepted by God, why did God allow him to die?

As people faced new challenges in those days, many believed the solution was to return to the beginning and start worshipping God. So we are told, "Then men began to call on the name of the LORD" (Genesis 4:26). Although men began to worship God, we know not all mankind worshipped the one and only wise God, the Creator of the heavens and the earth. Yet mankind worshipped. As we discussed earlier, what we believe in is what we ascribe our worship to. We need to discover within ourselves what we really believe in and trust. Is it ourselves, science and technology, the sun, moon, and stars, or the God who is the true source of life, the Creator of the heavens and the earth, the omnipotent, omnipresent, omniscient God, the Alpha and Omega, the unchangeable God? He is the one who has made us and given us life, and this is why we will all give account of our lives to Him. As Paul says, "So then each of us shall give account of himself to God" (Romans 14:12). We will be discussing accountability in chapter 4, but we hope and pray you will begin to appreciate the source of life right now.

Before mankind was put out of the garden of God, another order was in existence. This is the fourth order, the *order of willpower,* and it determines whether a person exists under the *order of light* or under the *order of darkness*. Which order are you operating under? As we will be discussing the *willpower order* of mankind, we hope you will be able to clearly see which of the orders influences or controls your life.

Because of the lack of knowledge on our part, we fail to acknowledge the order governing us. As we stated earlier, our unbelief does not erase these orders or change the fact that they exist. The state of mankind, with all its advancement, has committed plagiarism against God the Creator, who created us in His own image and likeness and gave us dominion over the birds of the air, the fish of the sea, and everything upon the earth. We might think we are doing a great job with this dominion but at what cost and under which of the orders are we operating: light or darkness?

2.4 Prayer Guide for Chapter 2

The purpose of the prayer guide is to bring us into the reality of this life we are living on the earth. The more sincere we are as we pray, the better the results we will experience. There are four categories of prayers designed for people at various stages of belief or unbelief. These stages are expressed as follows: (1) I do not believe there is a God; (2) I do not believe in one God and one way to God; (3) I believe in God but have backslidden; and (4) I believe and have faith in God. As your faith grows, you can move on to the next category of prayer you believe identifies with your faith in God. It is our prayer that by reading this book, you are making progress toward believing in the almighty God, the only true God, and are moving toward the last prayer: I believe and have faith in God.

2.4.1 I Do Not Believe There Is a God

If there is a God up there somewhere, I am speaking to You. You know I do not believe You exist or that You are God, who created the heaven and the earth and are watching over this earth that I live in. If it is true that You created this world we live in and it belongs to You, I apologize for not knowing and believing in You. Even though I have heard about You from those who call themselves Christians, I have not believed this is true and I still do not believe You are the only almighty God. If You are the Almighty, I give my heart to You as I continue reading this book. Let Your will be done for me to know You are God and You are out there, wherever you are. Amen.

2.4.2 I Do Not Believe in One God and One Way to God

I have been praying to You whose image is in my sanctified place I have made for You. I know You are a god, and I believe in You. Nevertheless, if You are higher and greater than any god I serve, I want to know You; I want to believe in You and in You alone. Forgive me for being ignorant when I could have heard about You. If You are the one and only God Almighty and there is none like You, through Your mercy open the eyes of my understanding and my heart to know You and to accept You as my God. As you open my heart, enable me to denounce all other gods and accept You alone as my God. Amen.

2.4.3 I Believe in God but Have Backslidden

O, my soul says, why have I backslidden from God's free grace? Is it because God has not been fair to me? I called out to God when I needed Him, and He did not come through for me. Why is my soul still longing for You? O, God, why didn't You answer me? Where were You when I called? Where were You when my life was in checkmate? My pain, grief, and hurt remain. I see the scars and feel the shame. How can I come back to God and ask God to come back to me? The scars have made me lose my way; the shame I feel is all that remains. Who is to blame—the One who cares for me, or me? I realize I've been deceived into blaming my God who watches over me. O, my soul, shouts out and says, "I thirst for grace that quenches within, the grace that brings Christ to me, to be my Lord and save me from shame." My soul is obsessed with pain; the hurts have possessed my brain; the scars are right before my eyes; and still my soul longs to be set free. God of grace and God of mercy, pardon me today, I plead; set me free in Jesus' name, and that I may live life once again. Amen.

2.4.4 I Believe and Have Faith in God

Father God, I thank You for saving me from the *order of darkness* and placing me under the *order of light,* which is in and through Jesus Christ, my Lord and Savior. Lord Jesus, may You always reign in and through my life. Father God, may Your grace keep me from falling into sin and keep me in your righteousness, which comes through Jesus Christ. Thank You, Father God, for opening the eyes of my understanding through this book to know the order I operate under will determine my final destination. Thank You, Jesus, for saving me from the *order of darkness* and for bringing me into and under the *order of light*. In Jesus' name I pray, amen.

Chapter Three

Not All That Glitters Is Gold

The Bible says, "Do not be deceived, God is not mocked; for whatever a man sows, that he will also reap" (Galatians 6:7). God cannot be fooled. Man, however, is easily deceived, and we all must remember that not all that glitters is gold. What do we mean by this expression?

"All that glitters is not gold" is a well-known saying meaning that not everything that looks precious or true turns out to be so. This can apply to persons, places, or things that promise to be more than they really are. It means everything that has a glamorous appearance isn't always good, valuable, or desirable.

> In real life, it is easier to apply the saying to situations than to items. For example, if someone appears to be your friend and treats you nice, this does not necessarily mean the person is really your friend and holds your best interests at heart. You can, of course, apply the expression to items or products. There may be situations where you have some product that seems to be identical to something else you have, but in reality, the new product you have is useless. So remember, when something seems too good to be true, all that glitters is not gold.[1]

Iron pyrite is a gold-colored mineral often called "fool's gold." To the untrained eye, pyrite has a sheen and hue that can easily be mistaken for the much more valuable metal, gold. Because the mineral does bear such a striking resemblance to gold, it has fooled many people—hence, the nickname of fool's gold. To the consternation of many miners, pyrite is often found in locations where gold is also present. This fooled many inexperienced miners attempting to build their fortunes during a gold rush, such as the well-known rush in California around the middle of the nineteenth century. Fool's gold is also a common term used to describe any item that has been believed by its owner to be far more valuable than it really is. For example, investing in hot stocks that seem too good to be true and prove to be exactly that can be referred to as investing in fool's gold.[2]

In 2000 I traveled to Ghana. Returning to Liberia, I came across someone selling chains he claimed to be made of gold. I was unaware there was something called fool's gold, so when I saw the chain, I was convinced it was real gold. I knew I could bargain with the tradesman and get the chain for a good price. I dickered with him, bought the chain, and proudly put it on my neck that evening. After a few weeks, the gold had changed and become like copper; it was unbelievable! Then I realized I had been deceived with what I later learned was fool's gold and not the real thing. After this experience, I promised myself not to buy any more gold. You may identify with this experience. People today are often deceived into buying fake items, imitations of the real things.

3.1 Mankind Deceived

The apostle Peter wrote, "Be sober, be vigilant; because your adversary the devil walks about like a roaring lion, seeking whom he may devour" (1 Peter 5:8). Many years ago Adam and Eve were deceived by our adversary, and mankind continues being deceived even today. Our failure to wake up from our slumber over the centuries has made it almost impossible for us to realize the fantasy world we live in and have pledged allegiance to. Taking into account his many years as king of Israel, Solomon, one of the richest and wisest of men, recorded this in the Bible: "'Vanity of vanities,' says the Preacher; 'Vanity of vanities, all is vanity'" (Ecclesiastes 1:2). The question that comes to mind is this: "What am I living for?" Or we could ask, "What is the purpose of this life?" If we look around us or even at our life and try to answer these questions, what can we say? Life is pain and suffering for some people. For others life is all about merrymaking, while for still others life is all about making ends meet while working and bringing up a family. For some, life is about becoming a celebrity, and for others it is all about war, enriching oneself by criminal means, or the escape offered by drugs and alcohol. Whatever our reason for living, we are in some sense to be commended, for at least we agree there's a reason for living.

Sadly, there are those who seem to have exhausted all reasons for living. They see no reason to be alive and thus contemplate or even follow through on committing suicide. Such people fall victim to the greatest deception of all: suicide as the solution. Do you want to be remembered as one who took his or her life? The one who takes his or her life is a fool of fools! This is the one who has given up, the one who refuses to look above, the one who has turned away from all possible options and, finally, the one who has given up on the source of life, namely, God. It is commendable for people to have enough hope in life that, whether they are doing the right thing or not, they want to stay alive. Only fools take their lives.

Does this mean we preach that dishonesty is being honorable? On the contrary, we reveal the hope of life that drives mankind within this universe, a hope that enables humans ultimately to see the real reason for living, unlike the one who falls prey to the greatest deception this life faces. Shall we encourage life even though a person lives in dishonor resulting in death? This is what Jesus said when He was called on to judge a woman found in adultery, which by law was punishable by death: "He who is without sin among you, let him throw a stone at her first" (John 8:7).

We believe life with hope in the true God is a secure life. It is said that young birds need not pray for feathers but for long life. With long life, eventually their feathers will grow. As long as there is life, there is hope.

This world we live in today was once occupied by others who were as deceived as people are today. To illustrate this deception, we are going to look at the life of King Solomon, from the time he was enthroned as king, to his becoming the greatest man in history in terms of wealth, wisdom, and honor, to his fall from grace because of the deception that came from his many foreign wives. Solomon was the son of King David, the man after God's heart. King David chose Solomon from among all his sons to be his successor to the throne. Talking to Zadok the priest, Nathan the prophet, and Benaiah the son of Jehoiada, King David said,

> "Take with you the servants of your lord, and have Solomon my son ride on my own mule, and take him down to Gihon. There let Zadok the priest and Nathan the prophet anoint him king over Israel; and blow the horn, and say, 'Long live King Solomon!' Then you shall come up after him, and he shall come and sit on my throne, and he shall be king in my place. For I have appointed him to be ruler over Israel and Judah." (1 Kings 1:33–35)

Sometimes I wonder if there is anything called selection, whereby we are selected to do a certain piece of work on the earth. When we take into account Solomon's selection, we are tempted to say there could be, even though we believe Solomon was chosen because he had the right heart and wanted to rule the children of Israel with wisdom and knowledge.

> On that night God appeared to Solomon, and said to him, "Ask! What shall I give you?" And Solomon said to God: "You have shown great mercy to David my father, and have made me king in his place. Now, O LORD God, let Your promise to David my father be established, for You have made me king over a people like the dust of the earth in multitude. Now give me wisdom and knowledge that I may go out and come in before this people; for who can judge this great people of Yours?" (2 Chronicles 1:7–10)

Solomon asked for wisdom and knowledge to rule God's people. And because he asked for wisdom to rule, God gave him not only wisdom but also wealth. What a generous God He is! God was with Solomon and blessed him mightily, and Solomon became the richest and wisest man of his time. You can read about the great wealth of King Solomon in 1 Kings 10:14–29, but we will use just a few extracts here.

> The weight of gold that came to Solomon yearly was six hundred and sixty-six talents of gold, besides that from the traveling merchants, from the income of traders, from all the kings of Arabia, and from the governors of the country. . .

> Now all the earth sought the presence of Solomon to hear his wisdom, which God had put in his heart. Each man brought his present: articles of silver and gold, garments, armour, spices, horses, and mules, at a set rate year by year. (1 Kings 10:14-15, 24)

We see the greatness of Solomon displayed in his massive wealth. Indeed, he was very rich, for silver was as common as stones. When the merchants came to the city, they paid taxes; some of Solomon's riches came from the countries his father David had conquered. He also obtained wealth from trading in horses and chariots. Because of the abundance of wealth, Solomon made gold shields to be used in special ceremonies. He also had a royal seat made where he sat to give laws and advice to the people of Israel and those who came to seek his wisdom. Even the dishes and cups in King Solomon's palace were of pure gold. Let's remember that Solomon asked God to give him wisdom and knowledge to rule the children of Israel. Because of this wise request, God blessed Solomon with wealth. But after all the wealth had been accumulated, what came next? The life of Solomon reveals what came next. Solomon set his heart on a quest to understand life and what it is all about. Is the purpose of life simply to eat and sleep, make merry, and die? What is life really about? Solomon wrote, "And I set my heart to know wisdom and to know madness and folly. I perceived that this also is grasping for the wind. For in much wisdom is much grief, and he who increases knowledge increases sorrow" (Ecclesiastes 1:17–18).

> When Solomon set off on his expedition to know wisdom, madness, and folly, he failed to realize his quest would separate him from God, a separation triggered by his many wives. The Bible says, "For it was so, when Solomon was old, that his wives turned his heart after other gods; and his heart was not loyal to the LORD his God, as was the heart of his father David" (1 Kings 11:4). At the end of Solomon's expedition, however, he gave his final report. In the end he understood what his true priority in this life should be and what life is all about. It is to be our priority as well: "Let us hear the conclusion of the whole matter: Fear God and keep His commandment, for this is man's all" (Ecclesiastes 12:13).

Solomon understood that life without God is meaningless and not worth living. All the wealth and fame, knowledge and degrees are meaningless without God. This is the bottom line to this life God has given us.

As we reflect on the account of Solomon, we learn about how we can set out our hearts to go after things we may see in life. Many people start with the right heart in their service to God, but where do they end? What is their present state? When we were growing up, we had great plans for our lives. But along the way, have we been diverted and lost track of where we were heading? If Solomon concluded that life without

God is meaningless, you can be sure he also gave us the way to live life and not die. We can choose to live by following the path Scripture sets forth for us, or we can remain in a hopeless state of mind and die without even trying to live. Hear what the apostle Paul said:

> I beseech you therefore, brethren, by the mercies of God, that you present your bodies a living sacrifice, holy, acceptable to God, which is your reasonable service. And do not be conformed to this world, but be transformed by the renewing of your mind, that you may prove what is that good and acceptable and perfect will of God. (Romans 12:1–2)

Like King Solomon, many of us live only for our present life. Nevertheless, King Solomon realized in the end that our primary purpose should be to fear God and keep His commandments and live.

What are we living for? I remember one day speaking to one of my brothers, who lives in the United States of America. He said to me, "Little brother, I took an inventory of my wages from the time I entered America, and I have accumulated over a million dollars, but I cannot see where the money has gone!" Can we relate to this? King Solomon could. He wrote, "I have seen all the works that are done under the sun; and indeed, all is vanity and grasping for the wind" (Ecclesiastes 1:14).

How many of us are trying to eat the crumbs off the king's table, and the more we try, the hungrier we become? This is because we are being deceived. We are chasing after the wind and becoming more frustrated in our pursuit. Do you sometimes ask yourself, "Why am I doing what I'm doing? Is my life improving or declining? Do I have a healthy relationship with family and friends?" It is time to start asking ourselves questions like these that will bring us into the reality of life and cut us off from the fantasy of Hollywood. There is hope in life, but it has to be cultivated by the giver of life, almighty God, the source of true peace.

Today, peace can supposedly come from many sources such as the United Nations (UN), the North Atlantic Treaty Organization (NATO), and the Economic Community of West African States (ECOWAS). Such organizations seek "world peace," but they and the peace they offer are deceptive. Let us briefly examine what the UN, NATO, and ECOWAS stand for in terms of peace.

> Peacekeeping by the United Nations is "a unique and dynamic instrument developed by the Organization as a way to help countries torn by conflict creates the conditions for lasting peace." ...
> Peacekeepers monitor and observe peace processes in post-conflict areas and assist ex-combatants in implementing the peace agreements they may have signed. Such assistance comes in many forms, including confidence-building measures, power-sharing arrangements, electoral support,

strengthening the rule of law, and economic and social development.³

How are NATO and ECOWAS involved in peacekeeping?

In cases where direct UN involvement is not considered appropriate or feasible, the [UN Security] Council authorizes regional organizations such as the NATO and ECOWAS or coalitions of willing countries to undertake peacekeeping or peace-enforcement tasks. NATO has been involved in active peacekeeping missions since 1994, and coordinates with UN Peacekeeping operations and directives. NATO was originally designated as a pre-organized alliance to fend off any hostility attempts originating in the Warsaw Pact countries.⁴

ECOWAS has been designated one of the five regional pillars of the African Economic Community (AEC). ECOWAS aims to promote co-operation and integration in economic, social and cultural activity, ultimately leading to the establishment of an economic and monetary union through the total integration of the national economies of member states. It also aims to raise the living standards of its peoples, maintain and enhance economic stability, foster relations among member states and contribute to the progress and development of the African Continent. ...

During the 1990s ECOWAS activities were increasingly dominated by its efforts to secure peace in Liberia, in particular through the involvement of ECOMOG (ECOWAS Cease-Fire Monitoring Group), which was dispatched to Liberia in August 1991.[5]

I recall during the conflict in Liberia, which escalated into a tribal war, ECOWAS/ECOMOG was sent in to preserve peace. Sadly, this is not what they did. They supported faction groups, made our sisters become harlots, and took some away to become their slave wives! Is this peace? The peace the world gives us is but for a while; it does not last. When there is no peace within, there will be no peace without. The greed of mankind limits the degree of peace we may experience, even though people may lay down their lives for that peace. Does this mean the peace we try to achieve is not worth our efforts? On the contrary, we speak of a better peace for mankind. At present the peace the world gives promotes selfish agendas, resulting in inequality in power and wealth.

Whatever we believe in—whether science, self, Muhammad, the sun, or the moon—if it does not bring us love, peace, joy, contentment, and freedom, then we need to stop believing in it. These virtues we call the five pillars of life enable us to experience lasting rest and true life from God in contrast to the temporary rest and deceptive life from the world. There is only One who can bring us into this place of rest, and He is the true God, our Lord and Savior Jesus Christ.

You may say, "I have love, joy, peace, contentment, and freedom in my life, but it is not through Jesus Christ." I say, "Check again, and come into the world of reality." Love, peace, joy, contentment, and freedom—these five elements of life that people need come only from the One who made all creatures, and His name is Jesus Christ. Jesus Christ is the Word of God; He was with God, and He is God. Listen to what the apostle John said by the revelation of the Holy Spirit.

> In the beginning was the Word, and the Word was with God, and the Word was God. He was in the beginning with God. All things were made through Him, and without Him nothing was made that were made. (John 1:1–3)

Let us now examine the five pillars of life.

3.1.1 The Five Pillars of Life

The five pillars of life enable one to live the true life that comes only from God and is given through His Son Jesus Christ. You can call what you have presently life, but that does not mean you have the true life that is from God.

If these pillars of life exist, then why don't we see them in all those who profess to be Christians? This is because some profess to be something they know they are not! Not all that glitters is gold. Today I can say to you that my life has been greatly affected through times of trials, but despite all that, I have enjoyed it. I must confess, though, this was not always the case. It was not until I began to receive understanding from the Lord that I began to stand firm in and display the five pillars of life. Although there will be trials and temptations, one who is in Jesus Christ can never lose these five pillars of life, which are the fruit of the Spirit (Galatians 5:22–23). Praise be to God. Let us examine each of these pillars separately. As we read, we will note what Jesus declared to His disciples about each of them.

3.1.1.1 The Pillar of Love

What is love? Love is (1) "a strong feeling of affection and sexual attraction for someone"; (2) "a great interest and pleasure in something"; or (3), in informal British English, "a friendly form of address."[6]

What is the Bible definition of love? "He who does not love does not know God, for God is love" (1 John 4:8). That is sweet and short: God is love. A friend and I were discussing this subject, and she defined love as being like the breeze that is felt but not seen. That blew my mind. Love is not quenched by distance. It is futile to command someone who is in love to stop loving or communicating with his or her loved ones.

We have this feeling that arises within us for a person or for a thing. This intangible feeling of love drives us to demonstrate our love through words or deeds, and it is awesome when we can truly manifest this feeling, cultivating affection and other emotions. Affection is not love but arises from love. The Bible says God is love. Love cultivates various emotional feelings such as affection, forgiveness, and others listed in 1 Corinthians 13. These we call the attributes of love or the cultivated emotions of love. They show different ways love can be expressed.

> Love suffers long and is kind; love does not envy; love does not parade itself, is not puffed up; does not behave rudely, does not seek its own, is not provoked, thinks no evil; does not rejoice in iniquity, but rejoices in the truth; bears all things, believes all things, hopes all things, endures all things. Love never fails. (1 Corinthians 13:4–8)

The apostle Paul tells us, "But God demonstrates His own love toward us, in that while we were still sinners, Christ died for us" (Romans 5:8). The Bible talks much about the demonstration of love. When we have love, these attributes of love are manifested in us and through us to others. While we were sinners, God proved His love to us by sending His only Son, Jesus Christ, to die for us. How many of us love our enemies? We were God's enemy, and He still loved us. This is true love! Jesus said, "Greater love has no one than this, than to lay down one's life for his friends" (John 15:13). This love Jesus demonstrated was not for His child or a relative but for a friend. What a love Jesus Christ demonstrated to us and for us! And it is this love we are to experience when we accept

Jesus Christ into our lives and operate under the *order of light* instead of the *order of darkness*. Praise be to God.

3.1.1.2 The Pillar of Peace

The English dictionary defines peace as (1) "freedom from disturbance; tranquility"; (2) "mental or emotional calm"; (3) "a state or period in which there is no war or a war has ended"; (4) "a treaty agreeing peace between warring states"; and/or (5) "the state of being free from civil disorder."[7]

When Jesus was preparing His disciples for His return to heaven, He said to them, "Peace I leave with you, My peace I give to you; not as the world gives do I give to you. Let not your heart be troubled, neither let it be afraid" (John 14:27). "Peace I leave with you," and "My peace I give to you." Allow me to say thank you, Jesus Christ, for this peace. Jesus spoke these words before He was crucified for our sins. He was with His disciples when He prophetically declared this blessing of peace upon them and those who would accept Him as their Lord and Savior. This peace is what the world is looking for, and it does not come through the UN, NATO, or ECOWAS/ECOMOG—it comes only through Jesus Christ. When Jesus spoke of the peace He gives, He was speaking of tranquility of the soul, an uninterrupted joy of mind, a peace that keeps one in the joy of the Lord, and everlasting friendship with God! Jesus Christ knew the world lacked peace. He knew His disciples were going to need peace to experience God's will on the earth as it is in heaven. These words were a legacy He was leaving with His disciples.

What a blessing to experience this pillar of life! The peace Jesus Christ gives is not like the peace the world gives. The Jews' salutations and benedictions of peace at the time of Jesus Christ were generally a matter of custom and ceremony, given without desire or design. When Jesus Christ said He gives peace not as the world gives, He was saying, "I mean every word I say; this is what I truly wish for you and will give to you." To His disciples He gives peace. And not only does He give it, but He also procures it, preserves it, and establishes it. He is the author of peace, the Prince of Peace, the demonstrator and promoter of peace, and the giver and keeper of peace. Jesus said to His disciples, "Neither let your heart be afraid." Why be afraid when you have the Prince of Peace with you?

The disaster of the world is for the world and not for us. Jesus Christ said, "I go to prepare a place for you, so that where I am there you may be also." He prayed for us as ones who are in the world but not part of the world. Doesn't it give you peace of mind, knowing this world is not your home and you are just passing through to go to the place that Jesus has prepared for you? We can say amen to that!

3.1.1.3   The Pillar of Joy

What is joy? Joy can be (1) "a feeling of great pleasure and happiness" or (2) "a thing that causes joy."[8]

Jesus said to His disciples, "Until now you have asked nothing in My name. Ask, and you will receive, that your joy may be full" (John 16:24).

I remember after deciding to follow Jesus Christ, I used to meet in a home with others for prayer and fasting every month. We even began to stay together, just to pray and fast and build up our relationship with God and with one another. I remember it as if it were today. One day in the prayer room during one of the prayer sessions, I set my face to the wall and began to pray. As I prayed intensely, I was taken up in the spirit and I saw the Lord Jesus Christ. As I was in the spirit, I heard the Lord say to me, "What is it you want? Ask that your joy may be full."

Oh my, an opportunity to become famous and rich! You name it. My desire was for the things of this world. I had a long list, as you can imagine. After naming all the things I thought at the time mattered for this life in Christ, I found myself back in the physical realm. In my spirit I felt something was wrong. I felt I had missed an opportunity to know and encounter God and to know the fullness of joy. Realizing this, I began to ask the Lord to forgive me. I told Him I no longer wanted those things I had asked for. I believe He did forgive me, and this is why I can now share with you this testimony.

Since then my prayer life has changed dramatically. No more do I want the things of this world but only Jesus. We sometimes do not know what to ask for, which is all right. But if we are willing to ask the Lord Jesus Christ, He can teach us how to pray and what to pray for so that our joy may be full.

3.1.1.4 The Pillar of Contentment

What is contentment? The English dictionary defines the word *contentment* as "a state of happiness and satisfaction."[9]

Jesus said, "The thief does not come except to steal, and to kill, and to destroy. I have come that they may have life, and that they may have it more abundantly" (John 10:10). Oh what a state to be in—happiness and satisfaction! When my prayer life changed to wanting to be like Jesus Christ more and more, I began to experience genuine contentment.

Speaking to the Ephesians, Paul said,

But you have not so learned Christ, if indeed you have heard Him and have been taught by Him, as the truth is in Jesus: that you put off, concerning your former conduct, the old man which grows corrupt according to the deceitful lusts, and be renewed in the spirit of your mind, and that you put on the new man which was created according to God, in true righteousness and holiness. (Ephesians 4:20–24)

The more we become like Jesus, the more we put on the new man, the image we were created in, and put off the old man, which is after the flesh. When we put on Christ Jesus, we actually understand the world we live in and the world we are a part of. It is not this world that is dominated and controlled by the *order of darkness*. We cannot reach this place of contentment outside of Christ Jesus. Jesus said the thief comes to steal, kill, and destroy. Who is the thief? The Devil, the leader of the *order of darkness*, is the thief. We do not need to ask whether he is accomplishing his task. We can see his full attack on mankind, resulting in a destructive way of life being accepted by mankind. What a deception! But Jesus said, "I have come that they may have life, and that they may have it more abundantly." That means contentment. How many of us are reaching out for this life of contentment in Christ Jesus? Sadly, there are very few. To live a life of contentment is one of the most beautiful experiences one can ever attain. And yet this is for the taking for all those who desire to be contented in this life.

      How beautiful it is when we put God in control of our life and are not controlled by others, or the advertisements on the television, or the things people say to get us to go along! When we have this pillar of contentment in our life, our state of life becomes admirable to many, and we will be the light of the world Jesus Christ spoke about in Matthew 5:14.

3.1.1.5   The Pillar of Freedom

      Finally, we come to the fifth pillar of life, the pillar of freedom.

What is freedom? *Freedom* means (1) "the power or right to act, speak, or think as one wants"; (2) the "absence of subjection to foreign domination or despotic government"; (3) "the power of self-determination attributed to the will; the quality of being independent of fate or necessity"; (4) "the state of not being imprisoned or enslaved"; (5) "the state of being unrestricted and able to move easily"; (6) "the unrestricted use of something"; or (7) "familiarity or openness in speech or behavior."[10]

The question we need to ask ourselves is this: "Am I free?" This is what the Word of God says concerning freedom: "Therefore if the Son makes you free, you shall be free indeed" (John 8:36). True freedom comes only from God through His Son Jesus Christ. The purpose of Jesus' suffering, death, burial, and resurrection was to secure our freedom from the bondage of the dark order and the power of sin. Through Jesus Christ we have become the righteousness of God and are able to fulfill the righteousness of the law and live as people of the light and not of darkness. If Jesus Christ lives in you, you are free. There is no condemnation to those who are in Jesus Christ (Romans 8:1) because our love for Him compels us to obey His words. Jesus said, "If you love me keep my commandments" (John 14:15). We can conquer the *order of darkness* by manifesting the kingdom of light *in* the kingdom of darkness! That is why the gospel of John records that "the light shines in the darkness, and the darkness did not comprehend it" (John 1:5). Whomever Jesus Christ sets free is free indeed. This pillar of freedom is yours for the taking. Thanks be to God we are free.

Having defined the individual pillars, let's get back to the five pillars of life as a whole. You may say, "I do not believe in Jesus Christ, and I don't believe He is the only way to obtain these five elements of life." That is deception! Does your unbelief change any of the orders that exist over mankind? Does your unbelief change your present status? Does your unbelief help you when you lack the five pillars of life? Does unbelief help anybody? There are some things we just cannot change, whether we believe in them or not, and this is one of them. The only thing your unbelief can do is to stop you from receiving these elements and from coming into the place of rest and the fullness of life. In the absence of these five life pillars, we are chasing after the wind, as Solomon said. I cannot emphasize this enough. We can fully enjoy love, peace, joy, contentment, and freedom only through Jesus Christ.

Are we deceived because we, who consider ourselves gods, find it humiliating to believe in anything outside of ourselves? Do we find it difficult to let go of that which we have believed in over the years? If this is the difficulty you are having, you are not alone. But you should be motivated to seek that which will transform your life and fulfill the desire of your heart to experience true life. This comes through Jesus Christ alone, as we saw in John 10:10.

The serpent's deception of Eve enables us to see the fourth order, which is the *willpower order* possessed by mankind. "Then the serpent said to the woman, 'You will not surely die. For God knows that in the day you eat of it your eyes will be opened, and you will be like God, knowing good and evil'" (Genesis 3:4–5). Willpower enables man to choose between the good and the evil—the light and the darkness. Mankind has the power to accept or reject deception. Sadly, we have been deceived and have continued to accept the deception over the years!

Let us look at this practical scenario. When you go into a store to get white bread, you find white bread on the shelf from four or five different providers. Which one do you choose? I ask myself this: "What is the purpose of the bread?" Is it not for eating and satisfying our hunger? When we begin to ask ourselves questions and answer them rationally, we are going to overcome deception. If you are buying things because of the advertisements you saw on the television, then you are living in a fantasy world. We will look at this more in section 3.2.

When employed, the power of the will within mankind enables the third order, the *dos-and-don'ts* order, to reveal the *order of darkness* and the *order of light*. What we purpose in our will to do manifests the other orders, which govern us whether or not we fully understand or believe this. As we see, Eve chose to obey the serpent's *order of dos,* which was against God's *order of don'ts*. Therefore Eve and Adam chose to disobey, and their disobedience manifested the *order of darkness*.

Let us go over this again, as it is very important we get it. Adam and Eve possessed the power to choose (willpower), and they chose to eat the fruit from the Tree of the Knowledge of Good and Evil, as directed by the serpent. In so choosing, they disobeyed God's "don't" (the third order). As a result, they turned from the *order of light* to the *order of darkness,* and this darkness is manifested in the world by mankind to this day.

> So when the woman saw that the tree was good for food, that it was pleasant to the eyes, and a tree desirable to make one wise, she took of its fruit and ate. She also gave to her husband with her, and he ate. (Genesis 3:6)

You will recall from the previous chapters that the lust of the eye played a role in making Eve desire the fruit of the tree and fall into sin. As a result, mankind was put out of the Garden of Eden and became even more vulnerable to the *order of darkness*. The *order of willpower* is triggered by self, and the self is who we are. The principles and values we live by originate from us. It is important for us to learn our lesson here. We need to begin to ask ourselves some questions that will help us make the right decisions and live realistically rather than trying to grab the wind. It is encouraging that we are in control of the fourth order, willpower. With the right questions and belief in the almighty God and our Lord Jesus Christ, our life is already in motion for promotion.

3.2 Deception a Way of Life Today

During His time here on earth, the followers of Christ said to Him,

> "Tell us, when will these things be? And what will be the sign of Your coming, and of the end of the age?" And Jesus answered and said to them: "Take heed that no one deceives you" (Matthew 24:3-4).

The heart of God in me cries out for the nations today to wake up from the world of fantasy and come into the world of reality by "hanging their hats where their hands can reach."

It is important to note that the first sign Christ Jesus gave to the disciples was a warning against deception. Indeed, Satan even tried to deceive Jesus to fall out of God's will for His life when he said to the Lord, "All these things I will give You if You will fall down and worship me" (Matthew 4:9). According to this Scripture, the wealth of this world is *controlled* by Satan; however, it is not *owned* by Satan. I'd rather be with the One who is the rightful owner of it all than the one who, through deception, has taken control of it all. This is why the apostle Paul, referring to Jesus Christ, revealed to us the difference between the owner and the controller:

> For by Him all things were created that are in heaven and that are on earth, visible and invisible, whether thrones or dominions or principalities or powers. All things were created through Him and for Him. (Colossians 1:16)

Do not forget that the fall of mankind gave that which was given to us initially to have dominion over to the control of the Devil. Satan could offer to Jesus only what was his to give, and he told Jesus he would give the world to Him in exchange for an act of worship. However, Jesus Christ, knowing who He was, did not bow to Satan's deception. We now appreciate why God said He will *give* us the wealth of the heathen as an inheritance. God takes from Satan, from the heathen, and gives to the believers. The Lord said, "Ask of Me, and I will give You the nations for Your inheritance, and the ends of the earth for Your possession" (Psalm 2:8). If only we could grasp who we can become in Jesus Christ, we would not embrace the deception of the world and the dark order!

When Adam and Eve chose to walk in disobedience to God by obeying the serpent and eating from the Tree of the Knowledge of Good and Evil, they turned over their authority and control to the *order of darkness*. That is why the Spirit of God revealed to the apostle Paul that the Devil is "the god of this age (world)." He wrote;

> But even if our gospel is veiled, it is veiled to those who are perishing, whose minds the god of this age has blinded, who do not

believe, lest the light of the gospel of the glory of Christ, who is the image of God, should shine on them. (2 Corinthians 4:3-4)

As the god of this world, the Devil has tremendous influence. Perhaps his greatest deception is convincing people that neither he nor God exists. Thus, such ideas as the big bang theory have come to prominence.

> The Big Bang theory is an effort to explain what happened at the very beginning of our universe. Discoveries in astronomy and physics have shown beyond a reasonable doubt that our universe did in fact have a beginning. Prior to that moment there was nothing; during and after that moment there was something: our universe. The big bang theory is an effort to explain what happened during and after that moment.
>
> According to the standard theory, our universe sprang into existence as "singularity" around 13.7 billion years ago. ... Our universe is thought to have begun as an infinitesimally small, infinitely hot, infinitely dense, something—a singularity. Where did it come from? We don't know. Why did it appear? We don't know.
>
> After its initial appearance, it apparently inflated (the "Big Bang"), expanded and cooled, going from very, very small and very, very hot, to the size and temperature

of our current universe. It continues to expand and cool to this day and we are inside of it: incredible creatures living on a unique planet, circling a beautiful star clustered together with several hundred billion other stars in a galaxy soaring through the cosmos, all of which is inside of an expanding universe that began as an infinitesimal singularity which appeared out of nowhere for reasons unknown. This is the Big Bang theory. ...

The singularity didn't appear *in* space; rather, space began inside of the singularity. Prior to the singularity, *nothing* existed, not space, time, matter, or energy—nothing. So where and in what did the singularity appear if not in space? We don't know. We don't know where it came from, why it's here, or even where it is. All we really know is that we are inside of it and at one time it didn't exist and neither did we.

Any discussion of the Big Bang theory would be incomplete without asking the question, what about God? This is because cosmogony (the study of the origin of the universe) is an area where science and theology meet. Creation was a supernatural event. That is, it took place outside of the natural realm. This fact begs the question: is there anything else which exists outside of the natural realm? Specifically, is there a master Architect out there? We know that this universe had a beginning. Was God the "First Cause"? We won't attempt to answer that question in this short article. We just ask the question: Does God Exist? [11]

The purpose of the big bang theory is to deny the work of the master Architect, as well as His very existence. As we read the article above, we can see that the big bang theory has no answers for some crucial questions. Where there is a question, I can assure you there is an answer, but we have to open our hearts to God for the answer. Remember, whether we believe it or not, things will not change that are already existing or in existence. We need to make room for and desire understanding that will awaken us from our slumber. If we fail to accept the knowledge that will awaken us from deception, then we will continue to live and die in this deception.

How many times have you heard people blame God for what happened to their father, mother, family, or friends? They may say when their loved ones were sick or in need, they prayed to God, and He refused to answer their prayer and did not heal or bring their loved ones back to life. Because of this, they deny God and turn their backs on Him. Or, perhaps when there are national or international disasters, we ask, "If there is a God, where is He? Why does God allow bad things to happen to us?" Many of us have this notion that God is our errand boy. When we call Him, He should come running and carry out our commands. Oh, what a generation without understanding and knowledge! This is deception, and we need to awaken from our ignorance.

What are we saying? We are saying that deception has blinded the eyes of our understanding, and we have turned our backs on the only hope we have in this life. We must accept the wisdom God speaks to us, for it reveals the one who has deceived us and turned us from God. Let us ask ourselves two questions. First, "Who is controlling this world?" Second, "If we believe in Jesus Christ, where is our home?" The answer to the first question is the Devil. As we saw in 2 Corinthians 4:4, he is called the "god of this age." The answer to the second question is heaven. Heaven is a place God has prepared for His people to live with Him. This is what Jesus said to His followers.

> "Let not your heart be troubled; you believe in God, believe also in Me. In My Father's house are many mansions; if it were not so, I would have told you. I go to prepare a place for you. And if I go and prepare a place for you, I will come again and receive you to Myself; that where I am, there you may be also." (John 14:1–3)

If our loved one is a believer in Jesus Christ and is at the point of death, we should be asking ourselves, "Why am I selfish and holding on to God's flower?" We sometimes forget that we no longer belong to ourselves. The apostle Paul said this of himself:

> For to me, to live is Christ, and to die is gain. But if I live on in the flesh, this will mean fruit from my labor; yet what I shall choose I cannot tell. For I am hard-pressed between the two, having a desire to depart and be with Christ, which is far better. (Philippians 1:21–23)

With his understanding of this life, Paul knew he would gain a greater life through death, for he would live eternally with Jesus Christ. If we are true believers in Jesus Christ, we know death simply means leaving this earth and going home where we belong—with our Lord and Savior Jesus Christ. Because of the Devil's deception, we become selfish and wish to refuse our loved ones who are in the Lord a joyful farewell. We need to awake from this deception.

In 2001, one of my sisters died from an illness. Before she died, she came to know the Lord Jesus Christ and started an orphanage. She took children from the streets of Liberia and gave them an education and a place to live. This work continues to this day. Before she died, I went to visit her. I was on my way from Monrovia, the capital of Liberia, on a mission to Grand Bassa County in Liberia. She told me, "I shall not die, but live, and declare the works of the LORD." These words are from Psalm 118:17. I joined her in prayer, according to her faith. While on my mission, I learned she held on as long as she could. When she was about to let go, her eyes opened in the spirit, and she saw our Lord Jesus Christ standing with an outstretched hand to her. God gave her the grace to share this testimony with the nurse before she went to sleep (died).

My senior pastor came to get me and give me the news that my sister had died. The night before I had been visited by the Lord, and I knew something had happened. When I saw the senior pastor, I was certain he had come with news about my sister's death. He tried keeping it from me for a while as we traveled back to Monrovia. Then I told him I had a feeling my sister was dead, and that was the icebreaker for him to tell me. My mom had come from the United States of America and was in Monrovia. When I got back and saw my mom, who also is a believer, we began to thank God for taking my sister home. Mom had anticipated that her little girl would bury her, but it was just the opposite. As she mourned for my sister, my mom shared that whenever she wanted to cry, the only thing that came out of her mouth was "Thank You, Lord."

I, on the other hand, had to preach at the thanksgiving service, and the Lord gave me a word that has changed my opinion about death and life. The word I received from the Lord was "going to a better place." I envied my sister because she was going home and seeing our Lord Jesus Christ, while I was left behind in this world of sin. We have a home that is not made by hands, yet many of us who call ourselves followers of Jesus Christ lust after this world and merely pretend heaven is our home. If heaven is our home, then why are so many of us afraid of death? Why do we hold on to life in this sinful world? I thought we are to receive death joyfully, knowing we are going home to a better place.

One day I said to the pastor of a church in Western Australia that this world is evil. He said to me, "No, there are good things still here on the earth to live for." Besides living for Christ Jesus, which is a constant battle with the dark order, what else is appealing to live for here on the earth? Because of the lust of the eye, Christians are being deceived and are going after the created instead of the Creator. We are accumulating wealth on the earth rather than wealth in heaven. It is God who has given us the earth on which to live and the beauty of the earth to behold, as well as mankind's creative inventions to admire. Are we to neglect and not appreciate the blessing of the earth to us? On the contrary, we preach of a place that is much better than the earth, where the streets are paved with pure gold and there is no death, sorrow, sickness, pain, or deceit. Let us take a glimpse at John's vision of heaven.

> And I heard a loud voice from heaven saying, "Behold, the tabernacle of God is with men, and He will dwell with them, and they shall be His people. God Himself will be with them and be their God. And God will wipe away every tear from their eyes; there shall be no more death, nor sorrow, nor crying. There shall be no more pain, for the former things have passed away." ... The twelve gates were twelve pearls: each individual gate was of one pearl. And the

street of the city was pure gold, like transparent glass. (Revelation 21:3–4, 21)

If the Devil is the god of this world and we are his followers, then why must God help us? Why should God save this world from disasters? Why should He prevent the massacres of adults and children and premeditated evil? Why would God interfere with the orders that are in existence before His chosen time? God is waiting for His divine and appointed time to come and judge the earth. The Word of God says, "To everything there is a season, a time for every purpose under heaven" (Ecclesiastes 3:1).

I am sorry to give you this bad news, but we are on our own. This is the truth of the matter. Unless we turn to God through faith in His Son Jesus Christ, we are definitely on our own, and there's nothing God will do about it. If God is who we say He is, the almighty, omnipotent, omnipresent, omniscient, and unchangeable God, then does this mean He must interfere with what is happening on the earth? If not, does this mean we preach a limited God who needs permission to do what is right for mankind, One who needs permission to save us from the Evil One? On the contrary, we reveal God's principles and God's attributes. God is holy and just, and these attributes set the boundaries. God is waiting for us to humble ourselves and seek His face. If we fail to do so, His judgment will come. Listen to Him: "If My people who are called by My name will humble themselves, and pray and seek My face, and turn from their wicked ways, then I will hear from heaven, and will forgive their sin and heal their land" (2 Chronicles 7:14).

This is what Jesus said concerning judgment when one man asked him to judge between him and his brother regarding their inheritance: "Man, who made Me a judge or an arbitrator over you?" (Luke 12:14). When Jesus Christ was on the earth, He separated Himself from the things of this earth. He refused to act as a judge concerning worldly possessions. Could Jesus Christ have rendered judgment in this case? Yes, He had the right to do so, but He refused because His kingdom was not an earthly kingdom but a heavenly one. We need to keep this in mind.

Do you see God as a wicked God because He does not prevent tragedies and evil? Do you see yourself as more righteous than the God who created you? Do you think your feelings for this world and for mankind exceed those of the One who gave you those feelings? Let us see what the Bible says. "The Lord is not slack concerning His promise, as some count slackness, but is longsuffering toward us, not willing that any should perish but that all should come to repentance" (2 Peter 3:9). And this is the question God puts to all of us: "'Do I have any pleasure at all that the wicked should die?' says the Lord GOD, 'and not that he should turn from his ways and live?'" (Ezekiel 18:23).

This is and always will be God's position. Because of His love for mankind, He is patient toward us and is giving us time to repent and come back to Him. If people will repent and turn to God, wake up from their slumber, and put God in control of their lives, things will be very different. Why are we blaming God and not ourselves for our self-centeredness and negligence? It grieves God to see the people He created in His own image and likeness (Genesis 1:27) turning their backs on Him, walking in the way of deception, and then blaming Him for the consequences they suffer. By the way, He can handle it. And, by the way, is our blaming and denying Him helping us?

Deception is a way of life today, and we don't even know it. It is destroying us and has enslaved us, even as we strive to achieve the deceptive dreams set before us. The Australian and the American dream is to own a home. People struggle and suffer to achieve this dream. A system has been put in place to facilitate the positive outcome of this dream, and we are encouraged to get on board. We board this dream world by taking a home loan mortgage. But to be approved for the loan, we must have a job and there must be some expectation that we will live x number of years. Is this not deception? How many people with home mortgages have lost their homes because they lost their jobs or the head of the household died? Is the dream of owning our own home good? Yes, but the way we often go about it is wrong. If we want to be sure everyone owns a home, we would have to put in place mechanisms that would guarantee lives and jobs for the duration of the mortgage. In the absence of this guarantee—which we cannot give—all is deception!

In making sure we do not lose our homes, insurance companies become the savior. When we lose our job, the insurance company fills in the gaps for our mortgage payments until we get another job. But this only adds to our debt. This also is deception. We have become slaves to credit cards and financial institutions, which have made us, believe we can achieve this dream world and acquire all that we desire. This is deception at its highest level!

We live in a world today that is full of actors. Our smiles, greetings, and conversations often are not real, and this too is deception. We arrived in Australia on September 1, 2006. We were contacted by the pastor of a church, and we were glad to go and visit the church that first Sunday. We were greeted warmly, and we made that church our home. Being from Africa and knowing the love and joy we share with each other when we meet in the marketplace or on the bus or on the streets, it was weird for me to see how one of the sisters of the church we were going to in Australia reacted when we saw her in the shopping center. She looked us in the eye and passed by without greeting us! I was taken aback by this, but it also happened with others from the same church. I could not believe what I saw and experienced repeatedly! Then I realized I was in what I call *a business world,* and even the church was a part of it. What a shame! In the Western countries, when you visit a service provider, someone greets you with a business smile and pretends to have an interest in you and your day. As you come to the end of your transaction, the business smile is quickly turned from you to the next customer or client. This also is deception. I always say in my heart when

I'm meeting someone, "Please don't give me a business smile; just a friendly one will do, thank you."

It is time we woke up from deception and faced the orders of the day. As we discussed earlier, our choices bring into play the third order, which is the *dos-and-don'ts order*, and this third order manifests the first two orders, the *order of darkness* and the *order of light*. Deception is a reflection of the *order of darkness,* and darkness is a part of evil. We will look at more of this in the upcoming section on the *power of good versus evil.*

Satan has deceived many, but how? The Bible says, "Satan himself transforms himself into an angel of light" (2 Corinthians 11:14). Why does he transform himself into an angel of light? Because mankind knows the light is good, and the Devil knows this. Satan, who is also called the Devil and Lucifer, was one of the masterpieces of God. He was beautifully made but fell because of pride. To him the Bible says, "Your heart was lifted up because of your beauty; you corrupted your wisdom for the sake of your splendor" (Ezekiel 28:17).

This is why the Devil is capable of transforming himself into an angel of light and at the same time deceiving us into believing we are truly living life as we should. You can decide to come out from under the *order of darkness,* or you can be complacent with your life and die without ever trying to live. I refuse to allow this to happen. I'd rather die trying to live than think I'm living when I'm dying.

Deception is from the *order of darkness*.

We need not be slaves of the darkness. Let us awaken from our sleep, and the *order of darkness* will not rule over us. When we are sleeping, our eyes are closed and shut off from the light. When we wake up, our eyes behold the light of day. In this same way, it is now time we awake from this sleep and begin to see the light that comes only through Jesus Christ. Jesus said, "I am the light of the world. He who follows Me shall not walk in darkness, but have the light of life" (John 8:12). Matthew also said of Jesus, "The people who sat in darkness have seen a great light, and upon those who sat in the region and shadow of death Light has dawned" (Matthew 4:16). Praise the Lord.

3.3   The Power of Good versus Evil

Jesus said, "That which is born of the flesh is flesh, and that which is born of the Spirit is spirit" (John 3:6).

> What is good and what is evil? *Good* means "that which is morally right; righteousness." It is something "to be desired or approved of."[12]

> On the other hand, *evil* is defined as "the force in nature that governs and gives rise to wickedness and sin."[13]

Whenever someone does the right thing, we commend the person by saying, "good man" or "good woman," "good boy" or "good girl."

However, when someone is not doing the right thing, we say that person is bad or evil or is doing evil. The words *good* and *evil* can be substituted for the *order of light* and the *order of darkness* respectively. The *order of dos and don'ts,* however, does not necessarily align with "good" and "evil." For example, Eve chose to obey the serpent's order of "dos," which was against God's order of "don'ts." Therefore Eve and Adam chose to disobey God, and their disobedience manifested the *order of darkness*. Similarly, your "dos" or "don'ts" can relate to either the *order of darkness* or to the *order of light*.

From the fall of mankind, when Adam and Eve were put out of the garden of God, both light and darkness have been manifested in the world. Because the *order of darkness* was embraced by mankind with a passion, God raised up a nation through Abram to bring judgment on those who were evil. To Abram (Abraham) God said, "I will make you a great nation; I will bless you. And make your name great; and you shall be a blessing. I will bless those who bless you, and I will curse him who curses you; and in you all the families of the earth shall be blessed" (Genesis 12:2–3).

Abraham fathered Isaac, and Isaac became the father of Esau and Jacob. The promise to Abraham was fulfilled through the descendants of Jacob (Israel). After four hundred and thirty years in Egypt, God visited Israel and brought them out of bondage by the hand of His servant Moses. "Moses and Aaron went in and told Pharaoh, 'Thus says the Lord God of Israel:

"Let My people go, that they may hold a feast to Me in the wilderness"'" (Exodus 5:1). God, who raised up Israel, was also the judge over Israel. This is why Moses told the children of Israel, "But it shall come to pass, if you do not obey the voice of the LORD your God, to observe carefully all His commandments and His statutes which I command you today, that all these curses will come upon you and overtake you" (Deuteronomy 28:15). Because of the dark order manifested by mankind, the Israelites failed to execute God's laws. As a result, God brought up individuals to execute His law and order. To the coming conqueror of Babylon, the Lord said, "You are My battle-axe and weapons of war: For with you I will break the nation in pieces; With you I will destroy kingdoms" (Jeremiah 51:20). Even though mankind falsely sits in judgment against one another, God will judge us all. Jesus warned, "Judge not, that you be not judged" (Matthew 7:1).

    The *order of darkness* has made this world a place of evil. Just think of the suicide bombers and those who carry out massacres and crash planes. Think of natural disasters and other accidents. These incidents do not choose special people or a special place. They do not say, "Today I'm going to get X, Y, or Z." They just occur, and those who find themselves in that place at that time suffer the destruction of property and sometimes loss of life. This is a world that takes life away from us, and that is the work of the Devil. Remember Jesus said, "The thief does not come except to steal, and to kill, and to destroy" (John 10:10). If we do not wake up from our slumber, we will die without even trying to live. The good and evil we see today coincide with the first and second orders, which are the manifestations of the *order of light* and the *order of darkness* respectively. If we agree, then we will have an understanding of what is happening all around us. We need to wake up from our slumber. This is the real issue.

    We cannot emphasize enough the respect we should have for others and their beliefs. In fact, because of the power of belief, we can be thankful people believe in something. The ability to believe could be used by God to save them. Because they believe, they might be led to ask, "If there is a God, what is the right way to God?" This, in turn, might give us the opportunity to point them to the one and only wise God who knows the heart of all mankind (Psalm 33:13). God has provided a way for mankind to know the way to Him, and He is able to bring them to Himself. Jesus said, "No one can come to Me unless the Father who sent Me draws him; and I will raise him up at the last day" (John 6:44).

    Nevertheless you—and all of mankind—have the responsibility to first believe. Believe what? Believe there is one God who is the almighty God. You must stop looking to and believing in other gods. Then you need to ask God the almighty to show you the way to Him. Why? This is to help us avoid confusion and deception in the world. I can assure you God loves you, and He will show you the way to Himself. If you believe this, you are not far from encountering Him. Jesus told His disciples, "As the Father loved Me, I also have loved you; abide in My love. If you keep My commandments, you will abide in My love, just as I have kept My Father's commandments and abide in His love" (John 15:9-10). I feel obliged to share this bold comment by our Lord and Savior Jesus Christ. In the midst of many diverse ideas, Jesus said clearly, "I am the way, the truth, and the life. No one comes to the Father except through Me" (John 14:6). Jesus Christ is the only one who boldly declared that He is the way. Believe me, He *is* the way.

Because of the evil in this world, Jesus Christ prayed to the Father for His disciples:

> "I have given them Your word; and the world has hated them because they are not of the world, just as I am not of the world. I do not pray that You should take them out of the world, but that You should keep them from the evil one. They are not of the world, just as I am not of the world." (John 17:14-16)

Jesus prayed that the Father would keep us from the Evil One. We need to ask ourselves this: "If we are not a part of this world, then what are we a part of?" Jesus gives us the answer: "Let not your heart be troubled; you believe in God, believe also in Me. In My Father's house are many mansions; if it were not so, I would have told you. I go to prepare a place for you. And if I go and prepare a place for you, I will come again and receive you to Myself; that where I am, there you may be also" (John 14:1-3). I repeat, if we fail to wake up from our slumber, *we will die having not tried to live. Jesus is the only way to life.* Only Jesus Christ can give us life in abundance. Jesus said, "I have come that they may have life and that they may have it more abundantly" (John 10:10). God said to mankind, "On the day you eat of the tree of the knowledge of good and evil, you will die." The death that occurred that day was spiritual death. When one is dead spiritually, that means he or she is separated from God. This is why Jesus said, "I have come that they may have life." This life Jesus was talking about is the spirit of mankind coming into oneness with God the Creator, who is the one and only almighty God. Jesus came to unite us with God the Father. The dark order is working against this. That is why we need to wake up from the deceit of the *order of darkness* and begin to live this life—a life worth living.

      The *order of darkness* controls this world and the entire world system and is the source of evil. However, believers in Jesus Christ have been given power that the dark order cannot comprehend. "In Him was life, and the life was the light of men. And the light shines in the darkness, and the darkness did not comprehend it" (John 1:4–5). This life, which is in Christ Jesus, enables believers to live holy lives while on the earth and to worship God. The way true believers in Jesus Christ live is beyond the understanding of the *order of darkness,* which manifests evil. If we are in Jesus Christ, we are in the light and are not part of the darkness. As Paul wrote, "You were once darkness, but now you are light in the Lord. Walk as children of light" (Ephesians 5:8). Clearly, good is related to light, and evil is related to darkness, for the apostle went on to write, "And have no fellowship with the unfruitful works of darkness, but rather expose them" (Ephesians 5:11). Thus, light also is related to God, and darkness is related to Satan, the Devil. The Bible says, "This is the message which we have heard from Him and declare to you, that God is light and in Him is no darkness at all" (1 John 1:5).

People may believe and do many commendable things, but it is most honorable and praiseworthy to believe in our Lord Jesus Christ. He is the One who awakens us from our sleep and gives us victory over sin and evil. "Thanks be to God, who gives us the victory through our Lord Jesus Christ" (1 Corinthians 15:57). Christ enables us to experience true life, which is the fulfillment of the five pillars (elements) of life: love, peace, joy, contentment, and freedom.

In the absence of the light of God in our lives, we cannot awake to the evil that has stolen this true life from us. You might say, "I do not need this life that comes through Jesus Christ; my life is full without Jesus Christ." I would urge you to examine yourself carefully in light of the fact that there is a greater Judge who will judge all mankind. The apostle Paul spoke of "the day when God will judge the secrets of men by Jesus Christ, according to [his] gospel" (Romans 2:16). You may or may not believe in the Judge who will judge all mankind. But consider this: If the world order demands accountability, will not the Creator of all mankind hold us all accountable for our deeds and actions? Does your unbelief change the orders that exist over and on the earth? Does your disagreement with policies made by world leaders change those policies? Keep all this in mind as you approach the next chapter. We will give account for every good and every evil thing we do.

3.4   Prayer Guide for Chapter 3

The purpose of the prayer guide is to bring us into the reality of this life we are living on the earth. The more sincere we are as we pray, the better the results we will experience. We present four categories of prayers designed for people at various stages of belief or unbelief. The various stages are expressed as follows: (1) I do not believe there is a God; (2) I do not believe in one God and one way to God; (3) I believe in God but have backslidden; and (4) I believe and have faith in God. As your faith grows, you can move on to the next category of prayer you believe identifies with your faith in God. It is our prayer that by reading this book, you are making progress toward believing in the almighty God, the only true God, and are moving toward the last prayer: I believe and have faith in God.

3.4.1 I Do Not Believe There Is a God

Being sincere with You, God, I don't want to believe in You because I like my life the way it is.

But because the prayer is a part of the book, I will pray it again.

If there is a God up there somewhere, I am speaking to You. You know I do not believe You exist or that You are God, who created the heaven and the earth and are watching over this earth that I live in. If it is true that You created this world we live in and it belongs to You, I apologize for not knowing and believing in You. Even though I have heard about You from those who call themselves Christians, I have not believed this is true and I still do not believe You are the only almighty God. If You are the Almighty, I give my heart to You as I continue reading this book. Let Your will be done for me to know You are God and You are out there, wherever You are. Amen.

3.4.2 I Do Not Believe in One God and One Way to God

If You are the almighty God, You know by now what is in my heart, and You know I'm not giving You the chance to reveal Yourself to me. You know all things I believe if You are the Almighty. Again, you know I have been praying to You whose image is in my sanctified place I have made for You. I know You are a god, and I believe in You. Nevertheless, if You are higher and greater than any god I serve, I want to know You; I want to believe in You and in You alone. Forgive me for being ignorant when I could have heard about You. If You are the one and only God Almighty and there is none like

You, through Your mercy open the eyes of my understanding and my heart to know You and to accept You as my God. As you open my heart, enable me to denounce all other gods and accept You alone as my God. Amen.

3.4.3 I Believe in God but Have Backslidden

O, my soul says, why have I backslidden from God's free grace? Is it because God has not been fair to me? I called out to God when I needed Him, and He did not come through for me. Why is my soul still longing for You? O, God, why didn't You answer me? Where were You when I called? Where were You when my life was in checkmate? My pain, grief, and hurt remain. I see the scars and feel the shame. How can I come back to God and ask God to come back to me? The scars have made me lose my way; the shame I feel is all that remains. Who is to blame—the One who cares for me, or me? I realize I've been deceived into blaming my God who watches over me. O, my soul, shout out and say, "I thirst for grace that quenches within, the grace that brings Christ to me, to be my Lord and save me from shame." My soul is obsessed with pain; the hurts have possessed my brain; the scars are right before my eyes, and still my soul longs to be set free. God of grace and God of mercy pardon me today, I plead; set me free in Jesus' name, that I may live life once again. Amen.

3.4.4 I Believe and Have Faith in God

Father God, I thank You for showing me that not all that glitters is gold. Father God, I ask you to forgive me for walking in deception and disobedience to Your Word. Father, I pray that the spirit of deception will no longer operate in my life, and I pray that my life will experience the five pillars of life. Father, I pray that the fruit of love will be manifested in and through my life, the fruit of joy will be manifested in and through my life, and the fruit of peace will be manifested in and through my life. Father God, may I experience contentment and freedom in my life. Father, I pray that my body will manifest good and not evil, in the name of Jesus, amen.

Not All That Glitters is Gold

CHAPTER FOUR

DOES LIFE AFTER DEATH ACTUALLY EXIST?

The Bible is clear: "It is appointed for men to die once, but after this the judgment" (Hebrews 9:27).

Christians and people of many other religions believe there is life after death. What do the scientists say?

> Death is only an interchange station between the two worlds. Every person at some point of his life questions himself what comes next after the physical death. Is everything to finish with the last breath or does the soul goes on living? ... The existence of soul is acknowledged by the people in Asia, Europe, America, Africa and Australia. ... In recent years the hypothesis of the soul occupying the heart has found certain confirmation. ... The heart controls the brain and not vice versa. Feelings, fears, dreams and thoughts are all decoded in heart cells. This *cell memory* [is] a soul.
>
> At the beginning of [2001], British scientists ... suggested that consciousness might continue living after the brain has stopped functioning. The research involved

63 patients that experienced clinical death. 56 people do not remember anything of the period when they were clinically dead. However, seven patients had clear memories of what they felt at that period. Four of them said they were overwhelmed with joy and peace and the time was running faster. Then they saw a bright light and saw mythical creatures that looked like angels or saints. They claimed they had been to another world for some time and then came back.

It is worth mentioning that none of the patients was religious. Three of them confessed that [they] did not attend church at all. Thus, these stories cannot be explained by religious fanaticism. ...

Later in December 2001 three Dutch scientists ... conducted ... research similar to those of the British scientists. [The scientists] claimed that the visions came at the very moment when the central neural system stopped functioning. This means that the consciousness is separate from the brain's activity. ... Dutch scientists also discovered that women had more powerful feelings than men. ... The visions of blind people do not differ from those who are able to see.

It looks like scientists are very busy with proving immortality of the soul. The only thing we can do is accept that death is only an interchange station between the two worlds.[1]

As we have said before, there are some things our unbelief just cannot change. The existence of life after death, along with the *order of light* and the *order of darkness,* remains. Because of the diversity of our beliefs, we may differ on this subject matter. We are accountable for our actions. And if this is so, then we must ask, "How and when are we held accountable? Does life after death actually exist?" When we begin to ask such questions, we are beginning to wake up to the reality of life and death in this world in which we live. If man believes he can get away with his deceptions and evil works through the *order of darkness,* he is deceiving himself.

What do you think will happen after you leave this earth? How surprised and disappointed in yourself will you be if indeed there is life after death? Again, unbelief will not change the fact, but it will keep you from preparing yourself for life after death.

When we speak of death, we understand it to be the moment when that which we call life leaves the body. Nevertheless, we are largely naïve regarding *spiritual* and *eternal* death, of which the Bible also speaks. If there are physical death, spiritual death, and eternal death, then there also must be physical life, spiritual life, and eternal life. In fact, the Bible speaks of these as well. You may not even be aware of these aspects of life and death, but they are present in the life of mankind.

What is *physical life*? The Bible says, "The LORD God formed man of the dust of the ground, and breathed into his nostrils the breath of life; and man became a living being" (Genesis 2:7). This is what physical life is: man becoming a living soul. The body and the soul became one. Physical life is that which encounters the tangible things of the earth and interacts with them. This is the life that grieves, feels love, joy, and peace, feels pain, cries, and feels the dying world. Why is this physical life important to us? Physical life enables us to enjoy this earth that God created. It is also through the physical life that the spiritual life functions and is housed. The physical life carries out the desires of the heart and thus manifests either the *order of darkness* or the *order of light*. Apart from a miracle, this physical life is experienced only once, and we have to account for what we do with it. Whether we manifest darkness or light, we are accountable for our actions.

What is *spiritual life*? Jesus said,

"That which is born of the flesh is flesh, and that which is born of the Spirit is spirit. Do not marvel that I said to you, 'You must be born again.' The wind blows where it wishes, and you hear the sound of it, but cannot tell where it comes from and where it goes. So is everyone who is born of the Spirit." (John 3:6–8)

Spiritual life is the heart of mankind coming into oneness with the Creator. This oneness enables mankind to worship and ascribe worship to God, who is our Creator. Being spiritually alive allows us to experience the five pillars of life (love, peace, joy, contentment, and freedom) and to experience true life, which comes through Jesus Christ. Spiritual life helps us to encounter and understand the world we live in today. When we have spiritual life from the source of life and the giver of life, our spirit life becomes natural and normal. This life causes us to grow into the ideal person we were meant to be. It energizes and motivates the self so that it can do all things through Jesus Christ, who strengthens us (Philippians 4:13). What an awesome feeling it is to be alive spiritually! There is no other guarantee we can have of a life full of love, peace, joy, contentment, and freedom outside of life in the spirit. And of this we can be sure: If we have spiritual life, we will experience the true life that comes with the five pillars of life.

What is *eternal life*? Jesus said,

"Let not your heart be troubled; you believe in God, believe also in Me. In My Father's house are many mansions; if it were not so, I would have told you. I go to prepare a place for you. And if I go and prepare a place for you, I will come again and receive you to Myself; that where I am, there you may be also." (John 14:1–3)

Eternal life is spending eternity with God and our Lord Jesus Christ.

Using a concordance, I looked up the literal Greek for [John 3:16–17] and here's what it says: *"For God loved the world on this wise (or after this manner): that he gave his only begotten son so that everyone who entrusts him will not be destroyed, but have life that continues through the ages (or Eternal life)!* The Greek word 'Apollumi – mean[s] "to be destroyed, to die, to perish, to lose or to mar. Let me stop here and say this is a REVELATION: The phrase 'eternal life' actually has two meanings. First, if you entrust your life to the sacrifice that Jesus made as being sufficient for ALL of your sins, He will give you the grace, hope and ability to live through all of the ages of your life without life destroying you or marring you! It literally says that! And second, if you entrust your life to the sacrifice that Jesus made for you, you will not be destroyed, but have life, or existence if you will, that is perpetual through every age there ever will be. There is no place where God ever limits the ages and says that Jesus' sacrifice will only provide life for us for 50 years, or two ages or 100 ages, or a million, etc.—He used the word "Aionios" to mean ALL OF THE AGES THAT WILL EVER EXIST ... whether or not your physical body has held up or expired—it means you will continue existing (your soul/spirit will). It doesn't mean your body will! That was never promised!

Just to look a bit at eternal life and death, we can see that the phrase 'eternal life' does not include hell. Hell, Sheol, Gehenna, and Abaddon—these are all synonyms for hell. Throughout the Bible, Hell is described as a place where we are separate from God, but conscious of ourselves and the wickedness that brought us there. God is saying that He sent Jesus to be our example to keep us out of that place of separation from Him! He also sent Him to count as our Sacrifice so we wouldn't have to go there! Such GRACE is beyond me to conceive that God would take a pure, perfect, sinless human and let His life count for my wretched life no matter how many times I sin is amazing. But that is what God SAID. What you are asking really is, "Is Jesus really our sacrifice for ALL of our sins, even if they number the thousands and tens of thousands? Can we still go to heaven?" Yes! The first part of John 3:16 makes it so very clear: God loved the world SO MUCH that He gave His only begotten Son. He was a Gift, THE GREAT GIFT. The Passover Lamb, slain from even the very foundation of the world and counting for everyone living until the very end of this earth, for every sin that will EVER be committed. That is what it says in the book of Revelation, and throughout the whole old and new testament.[2]

There are three aspects or stages of death: spiritual death, physical death, and eternal death. Let us examine each of them briefly.

What is *spiritual death*? It is the opposite of spiritual life; it is the heart of man not being in oneness with God the Creator. Spiritual death is manifested through darkness, or sin, as we can see today.

> When Jesus was hanging on the cross, He paid the price for us by dying on our behalf. Even though He is God, He still had to suffer the agony of a temporary separation from the Father due to the sin of the world He was carrying on the cross. After three hours of supernatural darkness, He cried, "My God, My God, why hast Thou forsaken Me?" (Mark 15:34). This spiritual separation from the Father was the result of the Son's taking our sins upon Himself. That's the impact of sin. Sin is the exact opposite of God, and God had to turn away from His own Son at that point in time.
>
> A man without Christ is spiritually dead. Paul describes it as "being alienated from the life of God" in Ephesians 4:18. (To be separated from life is the same as being dead.) The natural man, like Adam hiding in the garden, is isolated from God. When we are born again, the spiritual death is reversed. Before salvation, we are dead (spiritually), but Jesus gives us life. "And you He made alive, who were dead in trespasses and sins" (Ephesians 2:1).

> "When you were dead in your sins and in the uncircumcision of your sinful nature, God made you alive with Christ. He forgave us all our sins" (Colossians 2:13).
>
> The book of Revelation speaks of a "second death," which is a final (and eternal) separation from God. Only those who have never experienced new life in Christ will partake of the second death (Revelation 2:11; 20:6, 14; 21:8).[3]

What is *physical death*? This is the separation of the body from the soul. Physical death was the result of the sin of Adam and Eve.

What is *eternal death*? Eternal death is total separation from God forever, and that is something no one should ever want to be a part of.

> In short, eternal death is the fate that awaits all people who ultimately reject God, reject the gospel of His Son, Jesus Christ, and remain in their sin and disobedience. Physical death is a one-time experience. Eternal death, on the other hand, is everlasting. It is a death that continues through eternity, a spiritual death that is experienced on a continual basis. Just as spiritual life, by grace through faith in Christ (Ephesians 2:8–9) is everlasting life, eternal death is never-ending.

The most important question to be answered is "Does the Bible teach the doctrine of eternal death?" If the Bible doesn't teach eternal death, then we can pack up and go home because there is no further debate on the issue. God's Word, the Bible, is the infallible rule of faith and practice, and as such we must believe and teach only what it clearly teaches, and the Bible clearly teaches the doctrine of eternal death. We can point to several passages that explicitly state this, but for our purposes, only three will be needed, one from the Old Testament and two from the New.

- And many of those who sleep in the dust of the Earth shall awake, some to everlasting life, and some to shame and everlasting contempt (Daniel 12:2 ESV).

- And [the wicked] will go away into eternal punishment, but the righteous into eternal life (Matthew 25:46 ESV).

- And if anyone's name was not found written in the book of life, he was thrown into the lake of fire (Revelation 20:15 ESV). In verse 10, we are told that the Lake of Fire burns "forever and ever."

All three of these passages (and more could have been added) have as their main context the scene of final judgment. In other words, when Christ returns, three things will occur: 1) The general resurrection of "the living and the dead;" 2) the final judgment; and 3) the inauguration of the eternal state. Each of these passages demonstrates that during the final judgment of all people, Jesus will separate the righteous from the wicked. The righteous will be ushered into the final state of glory, while the wicked will be sent to the lake of fire for eternal punishment and torment. Note too (particularly in the Daniel and Matthew passages) that the same adjective ("everlasting" or "eternal") is used to modify both "life" and "punishment/contempt." What is true about one (life) must be true about the other (punishment) that both are eternal and last forever.

The doctrine of eternal death is not a popular doctrine to teach or proclaim. To do so often opens one up to scorn and ridicule. However, we must not let that detract us from what the Bible so clearly teaches; namely, that due to our being born in sin and trespasses, we are under the just condemnation of God for our sin. If we do not embrace the saving message of Jesus Christ, we will perish in our sin and trespasses and be under God's just judgment for our sin—eternal death. This is a sobering doctrine and requires the utmost care and compassion in its presentation.[4]

Let us look at the story of Lazarus and the rich man, which is recorded in the Word of God. This account will help us understand the three stages of eternal life and eternal death.

"There was a certain rich man who was clothed in purple and fine linen and fared sumptuously every day. But there was a certain beggar named Lazarus, full of sores, who was laid at his gate, desiring to be fed with the crumbs which fell from the rich man's table. Moreover the dogs came and licked his sores. So it was that the beggar died, and was carried by the angels to Abraham's bosom. The rich man also died and was buried. And being in torments in Hades, he lifted up his eyes and saw Abraham afar off and Lazarus in his bosom. "Then he cried and said, 'Father Abraham, have mercy on me, and send Lazarus that he may dip the tip of his finger in water and cool my tongue; for I am tormented in this flame.' But Abraham said, 'Son, remember that in your lifetime you received your good things, and likewise Lazarus evil things; but now he is comforted and you are tormented. And besides all this, between us and you there is a great gulf fixed, so that those who want to pass from here to you cannot, nor can those from there pass to us.' "Then he said, 'I beg you therefore, father, that you would send him to my father's house, for I have five brothers that he may testify to them, lest they also come to this place of torment.' Abraham said to him, 'They have Moses and the prophets; let them hear them.' And he said, 'No, father Abraham; but if one goes to them from the dead, they will repent.' But he said to him, 'If they do not hear Moses and the prophets, neither will they be persuaded though one rise from the dead.'" (Luke 16:19–31)

We can see that the rich man and Lazarus lived out their lives on the earth as normal people, one rich and one poor. The rich man seemingly had it all, while Lazarus was reduced to begging for food. After some time, both of them died, and they were taken to two separate places. What separated them? The lives they lived while on the earth—quite apart from their riches or poverty—separated them. The rich man asked for Lazarus to be sent back to his family to warn his brothers so they would not end up where he was. Many of us may be waiting for some sign to appear in the sky to warn us before we can accept the idea of eternal death. Or maybe we prefer to take our chances by not believing there is eternal death, which is eternal separation from God. We need to believe while we still have life.

Jesus said;

> "Not everyone who says to Me, 'Lord, Lord,' shall enter the kingdom of heaven, but he who does the will of My Father in heaven. Many will say to Me in that day, 'Lord, Lord, have we not prophesied in Your name, cast out demons in Your name, and done many wonders in Your name?' And then I will declare to them, 'I never knew you; depart from Me, you who practice lawlessness!'" (Matthew 7: 21–23)

Again Jesus said, "But the sons of the kingdom will be cast out into outer darkness. There will be weeping and gnashing of teeth" (Matthew 8:12).

As stated earlier, it is our responsibility to cultivate eternal life. Whatever we do with our physical life has an effect on the spiritual life, which also has an effect on our eternal life. In other words, the physical life you live on the earth determines your afterlife destination—whether you will enjoy eternal life with God or be eternally separated from God. As we have shared from the beginning, our unbelief cannot change what is already in motion. We can only fit in or stay out, and this is our choice.

You can underestimate this reality and refuse to adjust your life accordingly, but how regrettable it will be when you are faced with this reality! "If only I had known" will be the last words you will try to utter, but you won't because it will be too late! The author of Hebrews wrote, "Today, if you will hear His voice, do not harden your hearts" (Hebrews 4:7).

We also need to keep in mind the operation of the *order of darkness* and the *order of light*. After death there is life, and it is a time of accountability. It is our right to live the life we want to live now; however, in the afterlife we will be held accountable for how we lived our lives. It takes the Word of God to help us realize we are not on the right road to eternal life.

> For the word of God is living and powerful, and sharper than any two-edged sword, piercing even to the division of soul and spirit, and of joints and marrow, and is a discerner of the thoughts and intents of the heart. And there is no creature hidden from His sight, but all things are naked and open to the eyes of Him to whom we must give account. (Hebrews 4:12–13)

4.1 Why Did Adam Hide from God?

In the book of James, we read, "Do you not know that friendship with the world is enmity with God? Whoever therefore wants to be a friend of the world makes himself an enemy of God" (James 4:4). Since the fall of man in the Garden of Eden, mankind has been God's enemy, running away and hiding from God, the Creator. Man for the most part has not realized that the fourth order, *willpower,* enables him to choose what he possesses. It enables him to bring fully into manifestation either the *order of darkness* or the *order of light.* The *willpower order* gives mankind the opportunity to operate under the order of his choice. What does this mean? It means we have in our hands the power to manifest light and the power to manifest darkness.

Due to the lack of understanding over the years, mankind has believed his life is surrounded by two worlds, the world of good and the world of evil. Good people are those who obey the law and treat others well, while evil people are those who disobey the law and treat others poorly. But the world we see is blinded by the god of this age. Paul spoke of the people who have chosen darkness as those "whose minds the god of this age has blinded, who do not believe, lest the light of the gospel of the glory of Christ, who is the image of God, should shine on them" (2 Corinthians 4:4).

Because we have been blinded by the *order of darkness,* we find it hard to comprehend the worlds of good and evil. Many of us refuse to believe and accept the reality that exists over the earth. As we have discussed, though, our unbelief will not change this reality; it will only keep us from trying to learn more about how and why we do what we do. For example, consider the person who is a suicide bomber, one who believes that by killing others he or she will inherit heaven or paradise. How can people believe in this kind of deception and not even ask simple questions like "How can my doing evil result in my receiving a good reward?" and "How can my taking away the life of innocent people give me a place of peace?" As unbelievable as it is, those who carry out suicide bombings believe it will be well with them after they die! Let me assure you, they are in for a surprise—a surprise they will regret ever came their way. They will not escape the consequences of their actions because it will be too late. If we are accountable for our actions here on earth, believe me, they will give an account to their Creator after they have blown themselves up.

Because we have refused to accept the truth from the Creator, we are deceived into thinking we are gods. Let us wake up and think again. Do we think by having our way right now and denying the existence of the *order of light* and the *order of darkness* we can cause them not to exist? The *order of darkness* and the *order of light* are inevitable. Still, we have the willpower to choose what should happen in and over our lives. This power to choose, whether we choose the *order of darkness* or the *order of light,* is indeed a godlike power (see Psalm 82:6).

This fourth order, the willpower to choose, has its strength in, and manifests itself in, the physical realm. However, it is limited to the orders that exist in the spiritual realm, that is, the *order of light* and the *order of darkness.* We see this clearly in Genesis 3, when the serpent said to the woman, "For God knows that in the day you eat of it your eyes will be opened, and you will be like God, knowing good and evil" (Genesis 3:5). The choice in the physical realm had spiritual consequences. This is the satanic deception we spoke about earlier. Because of this deception, we are living in a world full of sorrows and pain, a world where we are deceived, frustrated, depressed, and killing one another under the selfish banner of "survival for the fittest." We live in a world where "globalization" dominates and is controlled by the wealthy nations. The depth of the deception becomes even more evident when we look at what these expressions actually mean.

The free dictionary by Farlex states that survival of the fittest is the "natural selection conceived of as a struggle for life in which only those organisms' best adapted to existing conditions are able to survive and reproduce."[5]

> On the other hand, world order globalization is a phenomenon of modern time in the last twenty years and center of the global processes because it affects all people and regions, directly or indirectly. ... Globalization is present in all areas of society, commerce, culture, science, technology and other fields. Globalization makes many changes that have taken place in all spheres of social life, and means all processes by which people all over the world are linked in a global society. ... It is an incomplete process in which the world becomes a place that leads to the intensification of relations between individuals, organizations and institutions at the global level, regardless of state borders.[6]

Does this mean we are spreading propaganda against globalization, science, and technology? On the contrary, we are merely revealing the deception promulgated by globalization under the banner of fairness.

Fairness is defined by the one who is the beneficiary and not by one who does not benefit. Mankind is experiencing imbalance because of the dark order under which he chooses to operate, and the dark order is controlled by the Devil. Injustice is the order of our day, and this will continue as long as we keep running away (like Adam) from the *order of light* and from our creator God. Globalization in itself is good, apart from mankind's greed and desire for power to control others and the world. If the world were being controlled by the *order of light*, globalization would benefit all mankind and not just the rich or those in high offices in our society.

We have the power to change our state of living for the good. This is always the platform of the politicians. When speaking to the masses, they sound as if they want to make our lives better, but often this is deception. When they try to make things better, they seem to end up putting us under greater oppression and complicating our lives. If we want to change our state of living for the good, we must consider the weak and the strong, the rich and the poor, the educated and the uneducated, the bound and the free. But no one wants to do this, so we find ourselves making more legislation that favors the rich at the expense of the masses. Our failure to run to the light and to God denies us the state of life for the good, so we continue to pursue the bad, showing that the order we are operating under is the *order of darkness.*

Adam said to God, "I heard Your voice in the garden, and I was afraid because I was naked; and I hid myself" (Genesis 3:10). It is still typical for us today to run and hide from our parents, friends, and authorities when we are guilty. We become fugitives running away from the law and from justice.

> In many jurisdictions, a fugitive loses the right to appeal any convictions or sentences imposed on him, since the act of fleeing is deemed to flout the court's authority.[7]

Charles Montaldo says this:

> When suspects who are accused of crimes decide to flee to avoid prosecution, they become the target of increased law enforcement efforts to locate them and bring them to justice.
>
> Many times law enforcement agencies ask the public's help in locating fugitives. Wanted posters are posted in public places, published in the media and on the Internet with photos of the suspects and the details of their crimes. One of the most effective ways to get the public's interest in these cases is to offer a reward.[8]

If criminals are afraid to go to prison or to be killed, then why do they do what they do? We need to think about this. Why would someone who knows what is right and what is wrong still decide to do the wrong thing and become a drug trafficker, a child abuser, a thief, a murderer, and so forth? Is it because that is what such people were born to become or because they inherited the "art" from their parents or grandparents? No, they were not born to be who they are; they choose to be what they are by selling out to the *order of darkness*. If you are guilty of wrongdoing and begin to regret what you have done, that is a good sign. It indicates there is still a conscience in you, and you are not being totally controlled by the *order of darkness*. And if you are willing, you can cross over to the *order of light*. Running or trying to hide from the light and from God will only make it harder for you.

If you turn on a light at night, the closer you are to the light, the more you can benefit from it. The farther you are from the light, the less the light benefits you. Jesus Christ is the light, and the closer you are to Him, the further the *order of darkness* is from you. When you become a fugitive, running from God, you become separated from the five pillars of life that come through Jesus Christ. This world offers only deceptive and short-term substitutes for the five pillars. The further you are from the light of God, the deeper you are in darkness. The more you run away from the light of God, the more you run into the darkness. On the other hand, the closer you are to the light of God, the further the darkness is from you.

In the case of Adam and Eve, God intervened when they sinned and made a provision for them before putting them out of the garden. In like manner, today God has made provision for us when we find ourselves walking in disobedience and under the influence of the *order of darkness.* Let us see in the following Scriptures how God has made provision for us when we sin.

> If we confess our sins, He is faithful and just to forgive us our sins and to cleanse us from all unrighteousness. (1 John 1:9)

This is how much God loves us, and if we are willing to read with a heart of repentance the next few Bible verses, we will become friends of God and not fugitives.

> If you confess with your mouth the Lord Jesus and believe in your heart that God has raised Him from the dead, you will be saved. For with the heart one believes unto righteousness, and with the mouth confession is made unto salvation. (Romans 10:9–10)

> [Jesus said,] "I have come that they may have life, and that they may have it more abundantly." (John 10:10)

> "For God so loved the world that He gave His only begotten Son, that whoever believes in Him should not perish but have everlasting life." (John 3:16)

> But as many as received Him, to them He gave the right to become children of God, to those who believe in His name. (John 1:12)

If you repent right now and ask Jesus Christ into your life, this is the first step to the light of God. The light is the only hope we have against the *order of darkness.* We know whenever light appears darkness disappears.

Why become a fugitive when eventually you will be caught? If not in this world, in the world to come you will face judgment. Why not stop being a fugitive and embrace this life and the light God gives out of love for you and receive the elements that come along with the light? Try it, and you will see what I'm talking about. Failing to act as a lawful citizen means you will have to give an account of your actions to the authorities. Fleeing as a fugitive only delays judgment and may make it worse. But when you are a law-abiding citizen, walking in the *order of light,* you do not need to give an account to anyone because you are doing what is right in the eyes of mankind. As the apostle Paul said,

> Whoever resists the authority resists the ordinance of God and those who resist will bring judgment on themselves. For rulers are not a terror to good works, but to evil. Do you want to be unafraid of the authority? Do what is good, and you will have praise from the same. (Romans 13:2–3)

All of us, however, will have to give an account to our creator God for the things we have done on this earth. Therefore, we need to be ready for this time, a time of accountability. Read more on accountability in the next section.

4.2 Accountability a Way of Life

What is accountability? *Accountability* is defined as "the obligation of an individual or organization to account for its activities, accept responsibility for them, and to disclose the results in a transparent manner. It also includes the responsibility for money or other entrusted property."[9] Jesus set forth the basic means of assuring we are always accountable when He said, "And just as you want men to do to you, you also do to them likewise" (Luke 6:31).

As we stated in the beginning of this chapter, we may not agree about life after death. We also may not agree on the three kinds of life and the three kinds of death that we talked about earlier in this chapter. But I think we will all agree that accountability is a way of life. Mankind is accountable, and people demand accountability from one another. We are going to discuss several areas in which accountability is required.

4.2.1 Family Accountability

Family accountability is usually carried out in the form of conversation. When everyone has come home from a busy day of working or schooling, the various family members give an account of how they spent their day. Other families may use different and more informal channels in accounting for their day, but verbal communication is an essential tool for family accountability. However, we must understand that the tongue (verbal communication) can be used to either build up or destroy a family. The Bible says concerning the tongue, "With it we bless our God and Father, and with it we curse men, who have been made in the similitude of God. Out of the same mouth proceed blessing and cursing. My brethren, these things ought not to be so" (James 3:9–10). I have seen families who use their tongues negatively, causing the family to become dysfunctional. If, for example, one of the family members does something wrong, wrong in its highest form, then the proper use of the tongue will unite and keep the family strong despite the wrong; but the misuse of the tongue to attack, criticize, and shame will tear the family apart.

The family also may be involved in budgeting and saving on a monthly, quarterly, or annual basis. So at set times they may take stock of their transactions, and the one in charge of keeping records will give a report to the others. In a family, the father, mother, and children are accountable to each other. However, society wants us to believe everyone has his or her own life to live. Because of this deception, many children have gone astray.

When I arrived in Australia with my wife and six children, we were so happy because of the opportunity to lead a better life. Within three years, my family foundation began to shake and fall apart. My oldest son decided to experience life for himself and left home. Our oldest daughter soon followed. As if this were not enough pain for me, in the fourth and fifth years after our arrival in Australia, our two other daughters, ages sixteen and eighteen, left the home. These actions came as a total blow to me. They destroyed me, even though I was still standing strong on the outside. The children have migrated into a new culture and society that believes everyone has to experience life personally no matter the age! Does this mean we blame the culture of our new country for what happened to our family? No, but we now understand and speak of the sudden challenges and changes families are not prepared to deal with. Instead of us as parents being helped by the government, the children were given youth allowance and support for accommodation after they left home! The government may not *cause* family division, but it essentially supports it and indirectly increases the possibility of our children getting involved in alcohol, drugs, and criminal practices. If family rights were protected for family members to be accountable to each other, we would have the community involved in bringing up the children and children obeying the community as they would obey their parents.

    We believe the authority of the parents has been restrained, leaving parents to only hope their children will grow up as responsible citizens in the society. Often parents are hurt within because of the lives they see their children living. Government needs to build a mechanism that allows children to be children and parents to be parents. In the current system, the children have taken the roles of the parents and the parents that of the children by obeying their children! We see many children today who have no regard for the elderly and their parents. What a world! Instead of child abuse being eradicated, it has escalated, and our children are now abusing themselves. My heart broke when I saw a twelve-year-old boy pick up a cigarette from the street to smoke! Oh how my heart cries out for these children! Is this the life we want to see our children living? It is for us to answer and decide. Is there a better way? There is always a better way, and it is the one we as a society have rejected and to which we refuse to turn.

The Bible says, "Children, obey your parents in the Lord, for this is right. 'Honour your father and mother,' which is the first commandment with promise: 'that it may be well with you and you may live long on the earth'" (Ephesians 6:1–3). When the government with good intentions desires to become parents for children to protect them from parents who abuse them, this is understandable. However, government policies have given children a life of adulthood before they become adults. This is why it is best for the government to work along with parents to help the children and not work with the children in the absence of their parents and without the blessing of their parents. In order for it to be well with the children, they need to respect their parents, and they will have long life. If parents are abusive to their children, those parents are operating under the *order of darkness*, and they need to stop and face the full hand of the law.

Most parents love their children. Mothers carry their young for nine months and go through the pain of labor to give birth to them. It is therefore right to acknowledge that the government's love for the children cannot surpass that of the mothers and fathers. The parents need to take the lead in guiding their children, backed by a government that seeks to help them raise and guide their young ones. Even a child who is difficult can be helped. The government's taking the driver's seat should not be the only way out. Jesus said, "With men this is impossible, but with God all things are possible" (Matthew 19:26). Family accountability is vital, not only for the family but also for the community and the nation.

4.2.2 Community Accountability

Birds of a feather flock together. Show me your friends, and I will tell you who you are. Such familiar statements speak of the importance of community. A community comprises homes that are occupied by families. It is not the homes or houses that define the community but the families or people who live in them.

I remember at the age of fourteen, I accompanied my older brother, who was seventeen at the time and some neighbor friends to the beach without any adults accompanying us. We stayed a bit late—till after five o'clock—knowing our parents came home from work at four o'clock in the afternoon. When our friends' parents got home, they began to ask where their children were. They soon learned their children were at the beach with my brother and me. When we got back from the beach, the parents of our friends called us along with their children and punished all of us. When our mother got home and was told about the incident, she also punished us and warned us not to go to the beach alone. I did not understand what was happening at the time. However, I know now I was being raised up in a village community. I wish my children had that experience, where people care for one another and not for themselves only.

4.2.3 Societal Accountability

We can give only what we have. In other words, we can produce only out what is in us. If we fail the family, we will also fail the community, and in turn we will fail the society of which we are a part. Nevertheless, because of deception, which is a way of life today, a family today can utterly fail but in the eyes of the community and the society be held up as an honorable and respectable family. The Bible says, "Do not be deceived, God is not mocked; for whatever a man sows, that he will also reap" (Galatians 6:7). We are accountable for our actions. Whatever we do, we will give account for it.

4.2.4 Domestic and National Accountability

"Let every soul be subject to the governing authorities. For there is no authority except from God, and the authorities that exist are appointed by God" (Romans 13:1). We are accountable to our leaders, but our leaders also are accountable to us. We are accountable to our leaders to obey the dos and don'ts of our nation. As long as we walk upright according to the laws, we have a good conscience, and we may even be pardoned should we commit a minor offense.

I was in church on a Sunday morning, and one of the sisters got up to testify. She thanked God for His grace and told how she was pulled over by the police for speeding through a sixty-kilometer-per-hour zone at seventy-five kilometers per hour. The policeman checked her record, and because her record was clean, he merely cautioned her to take note of her speed when driving. The policeman did not give her a ticket, which could have exceeded two hundred dollars.

Some of us have given up because of our past and refuse to start anew. But we all have to begin from somewhere. Even though the record is there, do not allow the past to keep you in it. Try to start anew, and in no time you will be proud of yourself, and others will be proud of you, because you are connected to the family, the community, and the society that make up the nation.

It is important to be accountable to our government. On the other hand, it is also important for the government to be accountable to us. This is simply good governance.

> Good governance is about the processes for making and implementing decisions. It's not about making 'correct' decisions, but about the best possible process for making those decisions. Good decision-making processes, and therefore good governance, share

several characteristics. All have a positive effect on various aspects of local government including consultation policies and practices, meeting procedures, service quality protocols, councilor and officer conduct, role clarification and good working relationships. The main characteristics of good governance are: accountability, transparency, following the rule of law, responsive, equitable, inclusive, effective, and efficient and participatory.[10]

Good governance, according to most politicians, is fixing and making things better. However, when politicians try to fix things, they often make them worse; and when they try to make them better, they usually make them harder, not on themselves but on the masses, that is, the taxpayers. As food for thought, let us taxpayers look at the comments below in relation to the recent American elections in 2012.

> We are again nearing election time and one thing you have to ask yourself is do politicians really care about you and your interests? Most of you will say well Democrats care for the little people who make less money and Republicans only care about the rich people.
>
> Both statements above are primarily true in the way that the parties are run. ... The question though is do either [of the] parties really care about how the country is run when it comes to the people's needs or are

they just in it for the money and title? If you really look at it from the angle that I recently saw then you might think otherwise!

This is what it boils down to. The United States is in debt for trillions of dollars and who is going to be paying that back assuming we get that far? If you answered taxpayers then you are absolutely correct! We the taxpayers will be paying almost every cent of that debt back in some way or form.

So what are these politicians doing about it? They are telling us that they have plans to pay it back. They are going to do this and do that and blah, blah, blah.[11]

When it comes to politicians, their plans of action are usually illusions and their promises to the masses fantasies. Greed and power in politics are driving forces behind legislation that is depressing the masses. Young people in their twenties are beginning to commit suicide; some carry out massacres. If we were really fixing and making things better, we would not be hearing of such things on the news. What is happening? What are we doing wrong or what should we be doing that we are not? Are these questions being asked by politicians, or do they not care because they consider the masses to be weak and failures in society?

I am not being judgmental of government but am speaking of things that often are invisible to politicians but very visible to the masses. People are dying and suffering because our politicians are dreaming of being the one in power to take the world to the next planet. This is deception that has blinded the eyes of our leaders and made us feel depression from the *order of darkness.* If we refuse to wake up from the politicians' delusions and fantasies, we will be among those who will die and not experience true life. Let us wake up so we can truly be free and experience the five pillars of life that are in Jesus Christ.

4.2.5 International and Global Accountability

> Global organisations affect people all around the world as never before, yet to many they remain distant, inaccessible and appear not to be listening to those they serve and affect. Our [One World Trust's] work to research and measure the accountability of organisations with global reach and influence aims to identify and publicize strengths and weaknesses in the accountability of global actors, demonstrate and define good accountability practice, enable cross-sector learning, and foster accountability reform of institutions involved in different ways in the provision of global public goods.[12]

Globalization is the new world order. Accountability, equality, and fair play purportedly form the umbrella that covers this order. But while the international policies of countries are based on their sovereignty, principles and values, economies, and military power, the policies of smaller countries are subject to being manipulated by superpower countries. Because of the support the smaller countries receive from the superpowers, they go along with these superpower countries' desires. A small country that fails to reconcile with the superpowers' expectations will suffer setbacks or even turmoil because the superpowers will end their support. This system makes the governments of small nations servants of the superpowers.

Just as small nations must be accountable to big nations, so it is that all human beings and nations, whether "big" or "small," have to be accountable to God. If the large superpower nations think they will escape accountability, they are mistaken. All of us will give an account of our lives to the source of life, God.

4.3 Accountability Instituted and Demanded by God

> That which has been is what will be, that which is done is what will be done, and there is nothing new under the sun. ... That which is has already been, and what is to be has already been; and God requires an account of what is past. (Ecclesiastes 1:9; 3:15)

So wrote Solomon, acknowledging that God demands accountability.

After creating mankind, God visited Adam and Eve in the garden during the cool of the day.

As in a family, the conversation channel was used to give account of their day. We can see clearly that God also used this channel later to get Adam's account of the day after Adam sinned. On that particular day, the account given by Adam did not please God, and we know God's reaction. So it is with all mankind. Whether you believe in the big bang theory, Muhammad, the goddess Diana, the true God through Jesus Christ, or no God at all, you, along with everyone else, will give an account of the life you have lived on the earth. Whether you believe this or not, you will have to give an account of your life to God.

But this you already know: We live in a world in which accountability is our way of life. This is a fact. If accountability is our way of life, then we need to think about this issue of being accountable to God. First, let us think for a moment of those suicide bombers who, in the name of *jihad* or whatever they believe, take their own lives and the lives of innocent people. Let us think for a moment of child abusers, child traffickers, those who carry out massacres, thieves, murderers, leaders who starve their own people, leaders who invade other innocent countries, and politicians who lie and cause uprisings. What happens to people who carry out such abominations? Think just for a minute about what happens to them when their life here on earth is over and they leave this world. Are they then free from the atrocities they committed while on the earth, never to suffer consequences for their acts? Think again. The Bible says this:

> Do not be deceived, God is not mocked; for whatever a man sows, that he will also reap. For he who sows to his flesh will of the flesh reap corruption, but he who sows to the Spirit will of the Spirit reap everlasting life. And let us not grow weary while doing good, for in due season we shall reap if we do not lose heart. (Galatians 6:7–9)

On the other hand, those who think they are the good guys and are righteous in their own eyes also will give account of their lives. See what Jesus said when someone called Him good: "Why do you call Me good? No one is good but One, that is, God" (Mark 10:18). Many who consider themselves "good" refuse to accept and believe the existence of the *order of darkness* and the *order of light* and that Jesus is the only way to God. They will have no excuse to give to God. Ignorance of the law is no excuse.

God has not hidden this information from us. The Bible says, "It is appointed for men to die once, but after this the judgment" (Hebrews 9:27). We are not just preaching religion here. We are simply revealing a truth we are living and helping others understand: After this life we will all give account to God.

This is how our Lord and Savior Jesus Christ put it in one of the prophetic parables He spoke to people of His day.

> "For the kingdom of heaven is like a man travelling to a far country, who called his

own servants and delivered his goods to them. And to one he gave five talents, to another two, and to another one, to each according to his own ability; and immediately he went on a journey. Then he who had received the five talents went and traded with them, and made another five talents. And likewise he who had received two gained two more also. But he who had received one went and dug in the ground, and hid his lord's money. After a long time the lord of those servants came and settled accounts with them.

"So he who had received five talents came and brought five other talents, saying, 'Lord, you delivered to me five talents; look, I have gained five more talents besides them.' His lord said to him, 'Well done, good and faithful servant; you were faithful over a few things, I will make you ruler over many things. Enter into the joy of your lord.' He also who had received two talents came and said, 'Lord, you delivered to me two talents; look, I have gained two more talents besides them.' His lord said to him, 'Well done, good and faithful servant; you have been faithful over a few things, I will make you ruler over many things. Enter into the joy of your lord.'

"Then he who had received the one talent came and said, 'Lord, I knew you to be a hard man, reaping where you have not sown, and gathering where you have not scattered seed. And I was afraid, and went and hid your talent in the ground. Look, there you have what is yours.'

"But his lord answered and said to him, 'You wicked and lazy servant, you knew that I reap where I have not sown, and gather where I have not scattered seed. So you ought to have deposited my money with the bankers, and at my coming I would have received back my own with interest. Therefore take the talent from him, and give it to him who has ten talents.

"'For to everyone who has, more will be given, and he will have abundance; but from him who does not have, even what he has will be taken away. And cast the unprofitable servant into the outer darkness. There will be weeping and gnashing of teeth.'" (Matthew 25:14–30)

Matthew Henry commented on this parable:

Christ keeps no servants to be idle: we have received our all from Him, and have nothing we can call our own except sin. Our receiving from Christ is in order to our working for Him. The manifestation of the Spirit is given to every man to profit all. The day of account comes at last. We must all be reckoned with as to what good we have got to our own souls, and have done to others, by the advantages we have enjoyed. It is not meant that the improving of natural powers can entitle a man to Divine grace. It is our liberty and privilege to be employed as Christ's servants, in promoting His glory, and the good of His people: the love of Christ constrains us to live no longer to our self, but to Him that died for us, and rose again. Those who think it impossible to please God, and in vain to serve him, will suffer loss like the man with the one talent. Such people complain that Christ requires of them more than they are capable of, and punishes them for what they cannot help. Whatever they may pretend, the fact is, they dislike the character and work of the Lord. The slothful servant is sentenced to be deprived of his talent. This may be applied to the blessings of this life; but rather to eternal life with God. Those who know not the day of their visitation shall have the things that belong to their peace hidden from their eyes. Their doom is, to be cast into outer darkness. This is a usual way of expressing the miseries of the damned in hell. Let us not envy sinners, or covet any of their perishing possessions.[13]

Does this mean we are now preaching Jesus Christ to the readers? Again, we share with our readers the Light of life-giving prophecy about accountability. This account is from one of the oldest and best-selling history books of all times. This book presents the past, the present, and the future of the earth and of mankind. This book is the Bible. You might say, "But I'm not a Christian, so I don't have to read the Bible." That is right—you don't have to. However, if you want to know what is happening in today's world and what the future holds, then grab a Bible and start reading it now. The Bible is not like other books authors write, trying to articulate their genius to us. The Bible is a one-of-a-kind book no one can fully describe. We are not merely promoting the Bible here; we are revealing the source of the information mankind needs to live and not die.

Why does mankind have to give an account to God? This is because God has given life to all mankind. Imagine a patient who goes to his or her doctor. The doctor carefully checks the patient and confirms the sickness already diagnosed by other doctors. Then the patient says, "I will not follow the instructions of the doctors because I do not believe them." What will happen to such a patient? He or she will suffer and die because of his or her unbelief! God is going to judge both the living and the dead. This is not a myth but a fact. Our only hope is to acknowledge this truth and turn to God in repentance and faith. The apostle John, being in the spirit, was enabled to see into the future and write of the coming judgment. He said,

> And I saw the dead, small and great, standing before God, and books were opened. And another book was opened, which is the Book of Life. And the dead were judged according to their works, by

the things which were written in the books. (Revelation 20:12)

Man's giving account of his deeds to God is like a woman with child who has to carry that pregnancy for nine months. When the fullness of time comes, the woman brings forth the child. We can choose to believe the woman will give birth or not. It is in our power to see what we want to see, to hear or feel what we want. But the fact is the woman is going to give birth as long as she is with child. So it is with mankind and God. In the fullness of time, God is coming to judge all mankind. We can choose what we want to believe, but that cannot change the inevitable, just as we cannot change what happens in the world today unless we begin to believe in the light. No matter what we do, we cannot and will not change this world and suddenly eliminate the violence and crime. We need to start trusting in the One who can change mankind and the world. Jesus Christ is the only One who can prepare us for this time of accountability before God. We will be looking more at this One in whom we need to trust to change our world and to prepare us for the time of accountability. As far as God is concerned, He is coming in the fullness of His time for all people to give account of their deeds. We need to know that it is not God's will that we perish. The apostle Peter said, "The Lord is not slack concerning His promise, as some count slackness, but is longsuffering toward us, not willing that any should perish but that all should come to repentance" (2 Peter 3:9).

God has made a way out for us through His Son Jesus Christ; we need only to receive and believe in Him. The Bible says, "For the wages of sin is death, but the gift of God is eternal life in Christ Jesus our Lord" (Romans 6:23) and "As many as received Him, to them He gave the right to become children of God, to those who believe in His name" (John 1:12). God is giving us the chance to believe in Him. Do you have the confidence that what you believe in will give you life after death and eternity with God? If your answer is yes, we commend you for your faith. On the other hand, if your answer is no or you're not sure, then allow us to recommend to you a more sure way to God, which is through Jesus Christ.

Jesus Christ openly declared He is the only way to God. He said, "I am the way, the truth, and the life. No one comes to the Father except through Me" (John 14:6). Furthermore, He said, "I will not leave you orphans; I will come to you" (John 14:18) and "Let not your heart be troubled; you believe in God, believe also in Me" (John 14:1). Further, still, He told his disciples concerning the Holy Spirit, "When He, the Spirit of truth, has come, He will guide you into all truth; for He will not speak on His own authority, but whatever He hears He will speak; and He will tell you things to come" (John 16:13). The apostle Paul later declared that it is through Jesus Christ we have access to the Father by the Spirit.

> For He Himself is our peace, who has made both one, and has broken down the middle

> wall of separation, having abolished in His flesh the enmity, that is, the law of commandments contained in ordinances, so as to create in Himself one new man from the two, thus making peace, and that He might reconcile them both to God in one body through the cross, thereby putting to death the enmity. And He came and preached peace to you who were afar off and to those who were near. For through Him we both have access by one Spirit to the Father. (Ephesians 2:14–18)

These words, and so many more you will come across as you read the Bible, confirm the certainty that Jesus Christ is the only way to God. You might believe in another way to God. If so, I urge you to examine again what the Bible says, and I encourage your quest for the only true God, the almighty God, the Creator of the heavens and the earth, the One who will judge all mankind. I implore you to ask Him for the way to Him, and I am persuaded you are not too far from finding the way if you seek Him with all your heart because He is near you. This is what God says. "And you will seek Me and find Me, when you search for Me with all your heart" (Jeremiah 29:13).

What should you do, then, to believe in God? The Bible says,

> The word is near you, in your mouth and in your heart" (that is, the word of faith which we preach): that if you confess with your mouth the Lord Jesus and believe in your

heart that God has raised Him from the dead, you will be saved. For with the heart one believes unto righteousness, and with the mouth confession is made unto salvation. (Romans 10:8–10)

God loves you and wants you to be with Him. He's speaking to you right now and showing you the true way to Him. What you need to do right now is ask Him into your life. Then ask Him to direct and guide you to others who believe in the true God like you. I believe right now God by His Holy Spirit is going to connect you with His body (other believers).

The season of accountability is just around the corner, and we have to be ready for it when it comes. Mankind has become delusional when it comes to God. There is great competition in the world today. Because of this competition, we have been deceived by the Devil into running programs in our churches at the expense of winning souls for God. This is why God's judgment begins with His children, the church. No matter what we believe in, we must not take accountability lightly. We will all give account of the life we have been given by God. Whether we are Christians, Muslims, Hindus, or Baha'is, or believe in some other god or in no god, we will give account of this life we have. Therefore, while we still have this life, it is time we believed in the true God. We need to take inventory of our life and how we are living. Remember, we have the power to choose, and we can choose the right way or the wrong way. But let us always remember, "Do not be deceived, God is not mocked; for whatever a man sows, that he will also reap" (Galatians 6:7).

4.4 Prayer Guide for Chapter 4

The purpose of the prayer guide is to bring us into the reality of this life we are living on the earth. The more sincere we are as we pray, the better the results we will experience. We present four categories of prayers designed for people at various stages of belief or unbelief. The various stages are expressed as follows: (1) I do not believe there is a God; (2) I do not believe in one God or one way to God; (3) I believe in God but have backslidden; and (4) I believe and have faith in God. As your faith grows, you can move on to the next category of prayer you believe identifies with your faith in God. It is our prayer that by reading this book, you are making progress toward believing in the almighty God, the only true God, and are moving toward the last prayer: I believe and have faith in God.

4.4.1 I Do Not Believe There Is a God

Repeat this prayer if your heart is leading you to do so.

Being sincere with You, I don't want to believe in You because I like my life the way it is. However, because the prayer is a part of the book, I will pray it again. If there is a God up there somewhere, I am speaking to You. You know I do not believe You exist or that You are God, who created the heaven and the earth and are watching over this earth I live in. If it is true that You created this world we live in and it belongs to You, I apologize for not knowing and believing in You. Even though I have heard about You from those who call themselves Christians, I have not believed this is true and I still do not believe You are the only almighty God. If You are the almighty God, I give my heart to You as I continue reading this book. Let Your will be done for me to know You are God and You are out there, wherever you are. Amen.

4.4.2 I Do Not Believe in One God and One Way to God

Repeat this prayer if your heart is leading you to do so.

Again, if You are the almighty God, You know by now what is in my heart, and You know I'm not giving You the chance to reveal Yourself to me. You know all things I believe if You are the Almighty. You know I have been praying to You whose image is in my sanctified place I have made for You. I know You are a god, and I believe in You. Nevertheless, if You are higher and greater than any god I serve, I want to know You, and I want to believe in You and in You alone. Forgive me for being ignorant when I could have heard about You. If You are the one and only God Almighty and there is none like You, through Your mercy open the eyes of my understanding and my heart to know You and to accept You as my God. As You open my heart, enable me to denounce all other gods and accept You alone as my God. Amen.

4.4.3 I Believe in God but Have Backslidden

Repeat this prayer if your heart is leading you to do so.

O, my soul says, why have I backslidden from God's free grace? Is it because God has not been fair to me? I called out to God when I needed Him, and He did not come through for me. Why is my soul still longing for You? O, God, why didn't You answer me? Where were You when I called? Where were You when my life was in checkmate? My pain, grief, and hurt remain. I see the scars and feel the shame. How can I come back to God and ask God to come back to me? The scars have made me lose my way; the shame I feel is all that remains. Who is to blame—the One who cares for me, or me? I realize I've been deceived into blaming my God who watches over me. O, my soul, shout out and say, "I thirst for grace that quenches within, the grace that brings Christ to me, to be my Lord and save me from shame." My soul is obsessed with pain; the hurts have possessed my brain; the scars are right before my eyes; and still my soul longs to be set free. God of grace and God of mercy, pardon me today, I plead; set me free in Jesus' name, and that I may live life once again. Amen.

4.4.4: I Believe and Have Faith in God

Father God, I believe and know life after death exists. Help me, oh Lord, to be prepared for this time. I know that I will have to give an account of my life here on earth. I pray that my report may be pleasing and acceptable to You. I believe and declare that my life is for Jesus Christ and my body is a slave for righteousness alone and will not be used for unrighteousness or for the *order of darkness,* In Jesus' name, I pray. Amen.

Chapter Five

Darkness and Light on the Earth

The apostle Paul made clear the relationship between darkness and light and where we as children of light should stand.

> Do not be unequally yoked together with unbelievers. For what fellowship has righteousness with lawlessness? And what communion has light with darkness? And what accord has Christ with Belial? Or what part has a believer with an unbeliever? And what agreement has the temple of God with idols? For you are the temple of the living God. As God has said: "I will dwell in them and walk among them. I will be their God, and they shall be My people." Therefore "Come out from among them and be separate, says the Lord. Do not touch what is unclean, and I will receive you. I will be a Father to you, and you shall be My sons and daughters, says the Lord Almighty." (2 Corinthians 6:14–18)

We have been discussing the various orders that are the powers operating on the earth. God revealed to Moses the beginning of the heavens and the earth [universe], and that beginning also revealed the existence of the *order of light* and the *order of darkness*.

> The earth [universe] was without form, and void; and darkness was on the face of the deep. And the Spirit of God was hovering over the face of the waters. Then God said, "Let there be light"; and there was light. And God saw the light that it was good; and God divided the light from the darkness. (Genesis 1:2–4)

At the end of each day of creation week, with the lone exception of the second day, God said what He created was good. When God had created the firmament, which is in three levels, darkness took over the second level of the firmament and possesses it to this day. God and the light dwell in the third level, and mankind lives under the first level. After God made mankind and gave him dominion over the earth, we know that because of the first two orders, the *order of light* and the *order of darkness,* the third order was instituted and put into motion by God over mankind. This is the *dos-and-don'ts order.* Man's failure to keep this order resulted in his being put out of the garden of God. Because of this sin, man also lost the dominion he had been given by God to the *order of darkness,* which has continued to control mankind even to this day, as most live according to their desires. *Until we wake up from the deception of the order of darkness, we will die without even trying to live.* Paul told the Roman Christians, "If you live according to the flesh you will die; but if by the Spirit you put to death the deeds of the body, you will live" (Romans 8:13).

The *order of darkness* is controlled by the Devil. This is why when he was tempting Jesus Christ, he could say to Him, "All these things I will give You if You will fall down and worship me" (Matthew 4:8-9). The Devil was referring to this earth. All was given to him when mankind chose to walk in disobedience and was put out of the Garden of Eden, the Garden of God. The truth is we are working on the Devil's plantation. This is why the world is what it is today. And, by the way, it will only get worse. The Devil controls this earth and everything in it. Whether we want to believe it or not, the *order of darkness* is in control of those who are not in the light and are of this earth. This is also why God, through His love for mankind, put into motion a plan to set man free from his bondage to the *order of darkness,* the bondage of sin and death. "I have come that they may have life and that they may have it more abundantly" (John 10:10), Jesus said.

Over the centuries, man has become content with the *order of darkness* reigning over him. But God's love for all people compelled Him to come in the flesh to redeem mankind. The Bible says, "God demonstrates His own love toward us, in that while we were still sinners, Christ died for us" (Romans 5:8). But many of us have rejected the love God has shown mankind. We are satisfied with the yoke of the darkness and continue to reject the light of God. This is why we raised the question of why God should help us or save us from disasters and the wickedness around us. Blaming God for our dilemmas or for what has happened to our loved ones or friends does not change the fact that these things have happened and will continue to happen, while the dark order has deceived us into blaming God for these bad things that happen to us. *Until we wake up from this deception, we will die without trying to live.*

Since I became a believer in the Lord Jesus Christ, it has not all been bread and butter. I have fallen at times, but I can say God has been faithful. In 2001 and 2002, I received a scholarship from a Bible school in the United States of America, and for two years I tried to get a visa at the American embassy in the Ivory Coast, West Africa. Twice I was denied a visa. On my third attempt, my mom, who was already in the US, decided to help me. She found someone to help me in the visa process and was sending him some money to do so. As I went to see this man for the first time, I was excited and felt it was the fullness of God's time for my life. After seeing him and at the same time praying, I began to become uncomfortable with the visa process, and I said, "This is not God. This is me trying to help myself." I then prayed and asked God to forgive me. I stopped going to the man for help with the visa process. I said, "If it is God's will for me, I will travel." Then I went to the US embassy in Ghana, West Africa, and was denied a visa again.

Because I trusted God so much, I said to God at the time, "God, I believe You can make it so I can travel overseas without a visa because you are God." Believe me; I believed God could do it. I still trust in God even today, but there came a time for my faith in God to be tested.

This test was carried out by the power of the dark order. The Devil believed he could stop me from trusting in God by way of reasoning or humiliation. The power of the dark order even used the Word of God to test me and set me up for failure so I would turn my back on God. He pointed me to Isaiah 7:9: "If you will not believe, surely you shall not be established." So what the Devil was telling me was, if I did not believe I could travel without a visa, then God would not establish me. You may say what I'm about to share with you is bizarre. But do not forget that the Word of God was being used by the dark powers to confirm that God was going to allow me to travel without a visa. Read Matthew 4:5-7.

    I guess you are saying, "Oh, fool!" Yes, I was a fool for my faith in God. I got an air ticket to travel to the US and went to the airport in Accra, Ghana, West Africa. At the end of the day, as you probably guessed, I could not travel to the country I wanted to visit without a visa. I was very disappointed and asked God, "Why?" This was just the beginning of the test. I wept bitterly before God and continued asking, "Why?" I left the airport and decided to spend the night in a hotel. While in the hotel, still weeping and questioning God, I felt the presence of the Devil and the dark forces in the room. They began to say to me, "Why did you trust God in the first place?" With many negative thoughts, the *order of darkness* began to speak to me. It was as if someone were with me in the room talking to me. I do not know where the strength came from. I sat at the foot of the bed and faced the chair in the room and addressed the dark order present in the room with me that night. I said, "Satan, God is God, and He's still in control." After saying this, the room felt free of the dark forces that had been speaking to me. This was in 2004.

In 2005 I had a vision in which the Lord Jesus Christ said to me, "Take the gospel to the other side." In 2006 my family and I arrived in Australia on a humanitarian visa. By the way, I did not see the visa until I was in the plane traveling to South Africa on my way to Australia. What I believed God could do, He did. Also, just for the record, I came along with seven members of my family.

> Now to Him who is able to do exceedingly abundantly above all that we ask or think, according to the power that works in us, to Him be glory in the church by Christ Jesus to all generations, forever and ever. Amen. (Ephesians 3:20–21)

God is God. If we put Him in control of our lives, He will be in control.

The *order of darkness* has dominion over mankind, and only the *order of light* will break us free. How foolish we are to believe we are free without the *order of light!* How can we think that? I had never felt depression until I arrived in Australia and took out a loan for a car through a finance company. I had to cry to the Lord to set me free. I was working, and my wife was also working, and this should have been a walk in the park for us. But this experience revealed the spirit controlling the financial companies, and it is very real. If you wish to experience depression, take a loan from a financial institution; then a month later, tell me how your life is doing with the stress that is beginning to build up and the pressure you are beginning to feel. Does this mean we discredit financial companies? No, we are simply revealing the yoke of the dark order that has enslaved us to the bondage of credit from which we are unable to break loose. Each one of us should try to live within our means and not borrow. As Christians, God tells us, "You shall lend to many nations, but you shall not borrow" (Deuteronomy 28:12).

We must stand against the dark order of the earth. When we receive the *order of light,* we are saying to the dark order, "I will not accept your lordship over my life." This means we are rebelling against the *order of darkness.* This is why when we become believers and are trusting in God, we are faced with the test of life. When the test comes, we need to keep on trusting in the *order of light,* which is always faithful. As the apostle Paul noted,

> "Whoever believes on Him will not be put to shame." For there is no distinction between Jew and Greek, for the same Lord over all is rich to all who call upon Him. For "whoever calls on the name of the Lord shall be saved." (Romans 10:11–13)

> And the psalmist prayed,

> To You, O LORD, I lift up my soul. O my God, I trust in You; let me not be ashamed; let not my enemies triumph over me. Indeed, let no one who waits on You be ashamed; let those be ashamed who deal treacherously without cause. (Psalm 25:1–3)

In the testimony I shared about the visa, I could have accepted that man's help to get me the visa I needed to travel. But by trusting in God, I was eventually able to travel with all my family. To God be the glory! If only we can trust the light that always prevails against the darkness, we will experience the true life that comes with the five elements this life needs: love, peace, joy, contentment, and freedom. God loves us, and He is waiting right now to help us if we are ready to trust in Jesus Christ, who is the head of the light order. Hear what the Bible says about Jesus: "In Him was life and the life was the light of men" (John 1:4).

If you are waiting to see a miraculous signs before you believe the *order of darkness* controls this earth, I can assure you time is running out, and you will die without trying to live. The quickest way to know the dark order reigns over the earth is to accept the head of the *order of light,* who is Jesus Christ. Then begin to read the Word of God, the Bible. Then proceed to do what God's Word says to you, and see what happens. The *order of light* and the *order of darkness* are reality and not fantasy. You can now choose to start living and not die by accepting the light that is able to break the dominion of the dark order from over your life. The apostle Paul said, "Sin shall not have dominion over you, for you are not under law but under grace" (Romans 6:14).

5.1 Darkness over and in Mankind

The Bible is the only book that explains to us the things happening in and around our lives. The New Testament of the Bible especially reveals the *order of darkness*. This is why the *order of darkness* discourages us from reading the New Testament and has caused some scholars to dilute the true meaning of its words. The Old Testament is even less read. This is how the *order of darkness* is progressing in its battle against the *order of light*. Specifically, the *order of darkness* has become a stumbling block to many in the church, stopping them from trusting in the *order of light* and carrying them away into darkness, far away from the light.

How can you know the dark order is over and in your life? The Bible tells us how the dark order is manifested.

> Now the works of the flesh are evident, which are: adultery, fornication, uncleanness, lewdness, idolatry, sorcery, hatred, contentions, jealousies, outbursts of wrath, selfish ambitions, dissensions, heresies, envy, murders, drunkenness, revelries, and the like; of which I tell you beforehand, just as I also told you in time past, that those who practice such things

will not inherit the kingdom of God. (Galatians 5:19–21)

Thus, the Bible speaks of the manifestation of the *order of darkness* as the works of the flesh. Why? Let's go back to the fall of mankind and see how the flesh came into play.

Genesis 3:6 tells us, "When the woman saw that the tree was good for food, that it was pleasant to the eyes, and a tree desirable to make one wise, she took of its fruit and ate. She also gave to her husband with her, and he ate." Lust starts from the desire of the flesh, and the Bible says, "That which is born of the flesh is flesh, and that which is born of the Spirit is spirit" (John 3:6). The *order of darkness* operates through the demands of the flesh, stealing from us contentment, one of the five pillars of life.

There is a difference, however, between the dark order operating *over us* and the dark order operating *in us*. Let us look at the two concepts.

5.1.1 The Order of Darkness Operating over Us

Moses, the servant of God, shows us clearly how the *order of darkness* operates over us in his account of the fall in Genesis.

> Now the serpent was more cunning than any beast of the field which the LORD God had made. And he said to the woman, "Has God indeed said, 'You shall not eat of every tree of the garden'?" And the woman said to the serpent, "We may eat the fruit of the

trees of the garden; but of the fruit of the tree which is in the midst of the garden, God has said, 'You shall not eat it, nor shall you touch it, lest you die.'" Then the serpent said to the woman, "You will not surely die. For God knows that in the day you eat of it your eyes will be opened, and you will be like God, knowing good and evil." So when the woman saw that the tree was good for food, that it was pleasant to the eyes, and a tree desirable to make one wise, she took of its fruit and ate. She also gave to her husband with her, and he ate. Then the eyes of both of them were opened, and they knew that they were naked; and they sewed fig leaves together and made themselves coverings. (Genesis 3:1–7)

The serpent (Satan) questioned Eve concerning the third order, the *dos-and-don'ts order,* and she responded to the question. Then the serpent directly contradicted God, telling the woman she would not surely die but would have her eyes opened to become like God, knowing good and evil. Often negative thoughts pass through our minds, suggesting that we do wrong things. This is a mystery hidden from mankind, but we get these thoughts, and more often than not, we act on them.

Imagine a person just wanting to hang out on a weekend. He reckons within himself, "I will just have a glass of beer and then quit." Because of this decision to have just a glass of beer, the person decides to drive to the pub. At the end of the day, the person finds he is too drunk to drive. Yet, even knowing he should not drive drunk, in this state of mind, the person finds himself taking the bait, saying, "I can do it. I can drive home. I don't need a taxi." As a result he may be caught by the police or, worse, involved in an accident. Let us just think for a moment here and ask ourselves how he got to this place—from just one glass of beer to being charged with drunk driving or being involved in an accident. Psychology might point us to the subconscious mind, but we say it is a mystery yet to be discovered. The Bible says, "The secret things belong to the LORD our God, but those things which are revealed belong to us and to our children forever, that we may do all the words of this law" (Deuteronomy 29:29).

    Often we hear people say, "I don't know how it happened. It was too quick." It is always too quick because there is no light to counteract the dark order. Even people who say the *order of light* operates over them struggle to overcome the dark order. History tells us that bishops, evangelists, and pastors have become victims of the dark order. I also have been a victim. All who are a part of the *order of light* can be victims of the dark order. The operation of the dark order over those who are not under the *order of light* is much more severe, for these people lack the power to win the battle over the dark order. "For the flesh lusts against the Spirit, and the Spirit against the flesh; and these are contrary to one another, so that you do not do the things that you wish" (Galatians 5:17).

    The Word of God reveals this battle as the war of the flesh against the spirit. The flesh is the slave of the *order of darkness*. In Australia, the government decided to help people stop smoking by putting gross graphics and warnings on cigarette packets. These graphics are designed to be so disgusting they will make the smoker want to quit smoking. A "quit line" number also is given on the cigarette packets, giving people a place to call anytime for help with quitting smoking. Despite all these efforts, people are smoking even more and progressing from mild forms of cigarettes to very strong ones. Smoking has become a lifestyle many people are not willing to surrender. Again, let's think for a moment. Smoking is bad for the health. We know it causes cancer, but people still go for what will kill them! People, what is happening here? We can try to justify this in some way, but the reality is that the *order of darkness* (Satan) reigns over us, and he's having his way with us as he chooses. Until we rise up and use the power we have to choose, which also can be enforced by the *order of light,* we stand no chance against the *order of darkness*.

5.1.2 The Order of Darkness Operating in Us

Luke, the physician, tells us that on the night before the crucifixion, "Satan entered Judas, surnamed Iscariot, who was numbered among the twelve. So he went his way and conferred with the chief priests and captains, how he might betray [Jesus] to them" (Luke 22:3–4). When the *order of darkness* is operating within a person, he or she is possessed and controlled by that dark order.

Earlier we talked about the suicide bombers, who murder innocent people. They are controlled by the *order of darkness*. Jesus said, "The thief does not come except to steal, and to kill, and to destroy" (John 10:10). The precise purpose of the Evil One is to steal, kill, and destroy. He is the head of the dark order, and he is fulfilling his mission through suicide bombers and any other people who choose to do his will. Because they are possessed by the *order of darkness,* they are gifted with deception by the dark order and are able to keep themselves composed, friendly, and even loving in order to fulfill the mission of their master. Let us keep in mind, the *order of darkness* has dominion over this world and is controlling the children of disobedience and has blinded them from seeing the light. The apostle Paul said,

> If our gospel is veiled, it is veiled to those who are perishing, whose minds the god of this age has blinded, who do not believe, lest the light of the gospel of the glory of Christ, who is the image of God, should shine on them. (2 Corinthians 4:3–4)

Why are people willing to blow themselves up? Is it because they have been brainwashed or because of their belief? The reality is that they are possessed and controlled by the *order of darkness*. There are other examples we could examine, such as people who are abusing drugs and alcohol. Illegal drugs are dangerous, yet people lay their lives on the line to have drugs. Even though they know if they are caught, they will go to prison, their families will be broken up, and they will lose everything, still they go after the drugs.

We human beings have five senses and think we know better than to go after things that will endanger our lives. But we take risks because we believe we are smarter than others, smarter than the law and able to pull it off. Such actions, however, do not prove we are smart but that we are being controlled by the *order of darkness,* which wants to destroy our lives. When we get to the place that we say to ourselves, "I don't care anymore," we know we have hit rock bottom. And this is where the *order of darkness* wants us to be in order to manipulate and destroy our lives. Do you think for a moment that the *order of darkness* cares what happens to you when you are caught by the law or when you die? No. But God cares, and He wants you to come to Him. "The Lord is not slack concerning His promise, as some count slackness, but is longsuffering toward us, not willing that any should perish but that all should come to repentance" (2 Peter 3:9).

We also see celebrities with all their fame and money being controlled by drugs and alcohol. Satan does not care about your fame. He cares only about how to steal, kill, and destroy you. Do not allow the *order of darkness* to destroy you. When you are finding it so hard to overcome drug and alcohol addiction, Satan will tell you to give up trying to quit. Next, he will tell you it is better to take your own life than to let the world see you in your present state. After you have taken your life, your friends and fans will speak glowing words about you. Does this mean we do not honor and respect celebrities who die tragic deaths? On the contrary, with passion we speak of the depressing scheme of the *order of darkness* that is bringing honorable people down with shame. You may believe me or not, but the dark order is trying to destroy us. The Devil knows he is bound for destruction, and he will take along with him all those who choose to believe his deception.

    With a heart of tears, we write this book. *Do not die without trying to live.* If you are under the control of the *order of darkness,* you have not started living life yet. You are still in darkness and have not come to the light. When you understand that *not all things that glitter are gold,* it will help you realize you are ignorant concerning the devices of the *order of darkness.* You need help to wake up from the deception of the dark order so you can begin to live a life worth living. Again, you might say, "But I am having fun living the life I live and doing what I do." But we will say, "All of us will give an account for the lives we live." We all have the power to choose. If you do not believe what you are seeing around the world today—that the *order of darkness* exists over and in mankind—then you need to ask yourself, "Who am I? Am I awake or asleep?" You need to do some self-evaluation.

5.2 Light over and in Mankind

"You are all sons of light and sons of the day. We are not of the night or of darkness" (1 Thessalonians 5:5), the apostle Paul wrote. And Jesus said, "Let your light so shine before men, that they may see your good works and glorify your Father in heaven" (Matthew 5:16). To understand this topic, we must go back to Genesis 1, where God said, "'Let there be light'; and there was light. And God saw the light that it was good; and God divided the light from the darkness" (Genesis 1:3-4). This was and still is the best thing that ever happened over the earth [universe]. Light is the opposite of darkness. When darkness is in a place and you light a match, what happens? The darkness automatically disappears; it "flees" from the light. When you turn off the light, what happens? The darkness returns. The light eliminates the darkness. The brighter the light becomes, the farther the darkness retreats—not from the one who is holding the light, but from the light that is being held.

Today, we who call ourselves Christians often seem to think we are light in ourselves, apart from the true light. But true light is found only in Jesus Christ, who said, "I am the light of the world. He who follows Me shall not walk in darkness, but have the light of life" (John 8:12).

When we do not have the true light, found only in Jesus Christ, then we Christians will be divided by various walls and have bondages among ourselves as a result of the darkness. The apostle Paul said, "We do not wrestle against flesh and blood, but against principalities, against powers, against the rulers of the darkness of this age, against spiritual hosts of wickedness in the heavenly places" (Ephesians 6:12). Our failure to comprehend this truth revealed to us in the Word of God—that we wrestle not against flesh and blood—has caused the Christian church to divide into many different denominations instead of being united as one in the love of Jesus Christ for the world through His suffering, death, and resurrection.

It is a shame to us Christians when we begin to see ourselves as Pentecostals, Catholics, Baptists, Full Gospels, and so on. Is Jesus Christ divided? Is Jesus Christ a denomination freak? Listen to His prayer for the believers as He was about to go back to the Father.

> "I do not pray for these alone, but also for those who will believe in Me through their word; that they all may be one, as You, Father, are in Me, and I in You; that they also may be one in Us, that the world may believe that You sent Me. And the glory which You gave Me I have given them, that they may be one just as We are one: I in them, and You in Me; that they may be made perfect in one, and that the world may know that You have sent Me, and have loved them as You have loved Me." (John 17:20–23)

Is Jesus proud of our doctrinal differences and carnality? What is Jesus concerned about? Jesus is concerned about being lifted up so that

He may draw all men unto the Father (John 12:32). This is what Jesus is concerned about—not our doctrinal carnalities. Does this mean we judge the church of which we are a part? On the contrary, we reveal the deceit of the dark order, which has caused the division of the body of our Lord and Savior Jesus Christ.

Because we are carriers of the light, we do not lead the light; instead, the light leads us. This we must always remember. When we arrived in Australia on September 1, 2006, we became part of a church that strongly believes baptism must be done in Jesus' name. I believe this, but I also believe that those who baptize in the name of God the Father, God the Son, and God the Holy Spirit are also baptizing in Jesus' name. If we believe Jesus and the Father and the Holy Spirit are One, then the people baptizing in the name of the Father, Son, and Holy Spirit are essentially saying, "I baptize you in the name of Jesus, Jesus, and Jesus. We must not allow the cunning deception of the *order of darkness* to divide the body of Christ over such matters. All who are doing the work of God in any form (including baptizing) should not be forbidden because they are on the Lord's side. See how Jesus dealt with a similar case presented to Him by His disciples.

> Now John answered Him, saying, "Teacher, we saw someone who does not follow us casting out demons in Your name, and we forbade him because he does not follow us."But Jesus said, "Do not forbid him, for no one who works a miracle in My name

can soon afterward speak evil of Me. For he who is not against us is on our side." (Mark 9: 38–40)

The apostles wanted to create a division, but what did Jesus say?

If the light is in you and over you, you will know that what is most important is holiness to God. The apostle Peter pointed the church toward holiness. He wrote, "As He who called you is holy, you also be holy in all your conduct, because it is written, 'Be holy, for I am holy'" (1 Peter 1:15–16). And Hebrews tells us, "Pursue peace with all people, and holiness, without which no one will see the Lord" (Hebrews 12:14). Another important thing is reaching perfection, as Jesus Christ pointed out: "Therefore you shall be perfect, just as your Father in heaven is perfect" (Matthew 5:48). Because we have failed in uniting on the most important issues (holiness and perfection), which will cause us to see God, we are divided on baptism, and speaking in tongues, and other issues. It is now time for the church of our Lord Jesus Christ to awake from our slumber. We need to stand together in oneness on the issues of perfection and holiness, without which no one will see God.

When the Gentiles were being added to the body of Christ, questions were raised about whether they too should be circumcised and keep the law as the Jews did. After much deliberation and many prayers by the council of the apostles in Jerusalem, this was their reply on the issue.

> For it seemed good to the Holy Spirit, and to us, to lay upon you no greater burden than these necessary things: that you abstain from things offered to idols, from blood, from things strangled, and from sexual immorality. If you keep yourselves from these, you will do well. (Acts 15:28-29)

In the early church, if salvation by faith in our Lord Jesus Christ was challenged by the claim that salvation is by works, they addressed the issue immediately. On the contrary, today we have churches that do not believe in holiness and encourage imperfection in the body of Christ. Is this really the church of light? A church that does not make Jesus Christ the center of its daily life will not be recognized by Jesus. He said,

> "Not everyone who says to Me, 'Lord, Lord,' shall enter the kingdom of heaven, but he who does the will of My Father in heaven. Many will say to Me in that day, 'Lord, Lord, have we not prophesied in Your name, cast out demons in Your name, and done many wonders in Your name?' And then I will declare to them, 'I never knew you; depart from Me, you who practice lawlessness!'" (Matthew 7:21-23)

Our Lord Jesus says that not all who call Him Lord will enter His kingdom. We need to put our house in order, for failure to do so will cause us regrets. Heaven will be full of surprises. Some people we do not expect to be there will be, while some who have been in church and supposedly doing the work of God may miss out. See what Jesus told religious leaders of His time: "Assuredly, I say to you that tax collectors and harlots enter the kingdom of God before you" (Matthew 21:31). Ask yourself this question: "Am I uniting the body of Christ Jesus, or am I dividing the body of Christ Jesus?" The way you honestly respond to that question will determine how you are judged when the time of judgment comes.

Light over mankind and light in mankind are two separate and distinct experiences. Instead of running away from the light, we should desire these two experiences.

5.2.1 Light over Mankind

"No one can come to Me unless the Father who sent Me draws him; and I will raise him up at the last day" (John 6:44), Jesus said. The purpose of the light is to bring mankind to God, and this means salvation.

What is salvation?

Salvation is deliverance from danger or suffering. To save is to deliver or protect. The word carries the idea of victory, health, or preservation. Sometimes, the Bible uses the words *saved* or *salvation* to refer to temporal, physical deliverance, such as

Paul's deliverance from prison (Philippians 1:19).

More often, the word "salvation" concerns an eternal, spiritual deliverance. When Paul told the Philippian jailer what he must do to be saved, he was referring to the jailer's eternal destiny (Acts 16:30–31). Jesus equated being saved with entering the kingdom of God (Matthew 19:24–25).[1]

In the book of Exodus we find that after God had brought the people of Israel out of Egypt, the pillar of fire in the night served as a light for them.

And the LORD went before them by day in a pillar of cloud to lead the way, and by night in a pillar of fire to give them light, so as to go by day and night. He did not take away the pillar of cloud by day or the pillar of fire by night from before the people. (Exodus 13:21–22)

The purpose of the pillar of cloud by day and the pillar of fire by night was to lead the way. The light we receive leads us to God. Without the light, we are lost; we do not know the way to God. Only Jesus Christ has the authority and power to bring us before God. When we have received salvation in Jesus Christ, then we move to the next level.

5.2.2 Light in Mankind

Concerning Jesus, the Word, the apostle John wrote, "In Him was life and the life was the light of men" (John 1:4). Over the years we have come across many Christians who say, "God loves me just as I am." How deceived we are! If God wants us to be as we are, why is the light of God in us? What is the purpose of salvation? If God loves us and wants us as we are, then why will there be a time of judgment and accountability? If we are in the church and are still carrying out the works of the flesh, which are the manifestation of the *order of darkness,* then that means the *order of darkness* still reigns over us. We can say or think what we want, but if we are producing evil, we are still under the *order of darkness,* and we will be cut off from God. Jesus said,

> "Even so, every good tree bears good fruit, but a bad tree bears bad fruit. A good tree cannot bear bad fruit, nor can a bad tree bear good fruit. Every tree that does not bear good fruit is cut down and thrown into the fire. Therefore by their fruits you will know them." (Matthew 7:17–20)

If in the beginning of the world, God separated the *order of darkness* from the *order of light,* then there is no way darkness and light will work together.

Often we hear people say, "I'm a sinner (one who is under the *order of darkness*), but God always answers my prayers." Is it God who is answering that prayer that produces dishonesty or the working of the *order of darkness*? You need to think again. There is no middle ground here. I came across a pastor (actually I worked with him for a while) who says, "I'm from a Baptist background, and I was baptized in the Holy Spirit with the evidence of speaking in tongues; therefore, I have encountered Pentecost. I'm going to be in the middle." I repeat: there is no middle ground. You are either for the *order of light* or for the *order of darkness*. Those of us who go to church and know the truth but are not applying the truth in our lives will regret taking God's love for us for granted. If we are willing to obey and trust God, He will help in our Christian journey, and nothing shall separate us from His love—except sin. Speaking of God's love, the apostle Paul said this:

> In all these things we are more than conquerors through Him who loved us. For I am persuaded that neither death nor life, nor angels nor principalities nor powers, nor things present nor things to come, nor height nor depth, nor any other created thing, shall be able to separate us from the love of God which is in Christ Jesus our Lord. (Romans 8:37–39)

However, when we sin, we separate ourselves from God and so do not experience His love, although His love is still there. Let no one deceive you. I call you today to strive toward God in holiness and perfection. As the apostle Paul told the Philippian Christians, "Work out your own salvation with fear and trembling; for it is God who works in you both to will and to do for His good pleasure" (Philippians 2:12–13).

Let's look at the parable of the ten virgins and see what we can learn from it.

> "Then the kingdom of heaven shall be likened to ten virgins who took their lamps and went out to meet the bridegroom. Now five of them were wise, and five were foolish. Those that were foolish took their lamps and took no oil with them, but the wise took oil in their vessels with their lamps. But while the bridegroom was delayed, they all slumbered and slept. And at midnight a cry was heard: 'Behold, the bridegroom is coming; go out to meet him!' Then all those virgins arose and trimmed their lamps. And the foolish said to the wise, 'Give us some of your oil, for our lamps are going out.' But the wise answered, saying, 'No, lest there should not be enough for us and you; but go rather to those who sell, and buy for yourselves.' And while they went to buy, the bridegroom came, and those who were ready went in with him to the wedding; and the door was shut. Afterward the other virgins came also, saying, 'Lord, Lord, open to us!' But he answered and said, 'Assuredly, I say to you, I do not know you.' Watch therefore, for you know neither the day nor the hour in which the Son of Man is coming." (Matthew 25:1-13)

This parable is one of several prophetic parables, so classified because they speak of things yet to take place. This parable reveals the importance of being ready for Christ and the rapture that will take us to the Bridegroom. Now the first thing we need to consider in this parable is the people. The Bible says there were ten of them and they were all virgins. If they were all virgins, that means they did what was right in the sight of God. They appear to have been under the *order of light* and doing what was right. They were like people in our time who are doing good works and obeying the law. Next, the parable talks about lamps and oil. The ten virgins had lamps and oil within their lamps. But only five of them took along extra oil to carry them all night, while the other five assumed the oil in their lamps was sufficient and they needed no more. This is a revelation: They did what was right almost up to the time of the coming of the bridegroom.

Think about this for a minute and ask yourself what went wrong. Think also of these words of wise King Solomon: "I returned and saw under the sun that— The race is not to the swift, nor the battle to the strong, nor bread to the wise, nor riches to men of understanding, nor favor to men of skill; but time and chance happen to them all" (Ecclesiastes 9:11). And when speaking about the end time to His disciples, Jesus said, "He who endures to the end shall be saved" (Matthew 24:13).

Let no one deceive you. After you have given your life to God, He expects you to change and be conformed to Jesus Christ. You should never excuse your behavior by saying, "God loves me as I am" or "God understands." Do not let anyone or anything encourage you to remain in sin and under the *order of darkness*. After you have given your life to Jesus, you are to conform to the image of Jesus Christ, the Son of God (Romans 8:29). Whatever you may be going through that is stopping you from being the true light of God on this earth, it is now time for you to challenge yourself. Begin to see yourself as God has destined you to be according to His Word. This is why we have the light in us. The purpose of the light in us is to bring us into the full image of God's Son, Jesus Christ. This light is to make us like Jesus.

    I shared Jesus with a friend once, and her life changed from then on. This friend would go dancing and enjoyed strong drinks. She could not see anything wrong with her life. Many Christians are involved in things that dim their light, and they are wondering why they are not experiencing more of the light of God. I said to this friend, "When you drink the strong drinks or go dancing, do you do it unto Jesus Christ?" She said no. If what we do is not unto our Lord and Savior Jesus Christ, then for whom are we doing it? From that day she purposed in her heart to do all things unto the Lord Jesus Christ. This is the light in us. Our lives are to manifest Christ and Him alone. If we are not doing that, we are not shining the light but are being deceived.

    If you are a Christian, whatever you are doing should be unto our Lord Jesus Christ. If you are not doing it for Him, you are not to do it at all, because you are not your own but belong to God. The apostle Paul reminded the Corinthian Christians of this important truth:

> Do you not know that your body is the temple of the Holy Spirit who is in you, whom you have from God, and you are not your own? For you were bought at a price; therefore glorify God in your body and in your spirit, which are God's. (1 Corinthians 6:19–20)

When we find ourselves doing things that are not unto, or honoring, Jesus Christ, we should know that the light in us is becoming dimmer and dimmer, and we will soon lose our way. When we allow the light within us to have its way, we will begin to realize how we have been deceived by the *order of darkness*. The *order of darkness* makes us believe this world and everything in it is what we should live for. We then try working hard to get everything we want in this world, and when we cannot, we become frustrated in this process. The light is responsible for bringing us to the fullness of our purpose here on earth and enabling us to fulfill it. The light also shows us, through God's Word, the home that awaits us. To God be the glory!

5.3 Personal Evaluation

We began this conversation by sharing how it all began and revealing the battles we face. We will look at some of these battles again and this time becomes a bit more personal. We will evaluate ourselves to help us determine which of the orders is operating over or in our lives, the *order of light* or the *order of darkness*. In this regard, we will look at the battle of pride, the battle of lust, and the battle of self.

5.3.1 The Battle of Pride

Here we will use Jesus' parable of the prodigal son. In this parable the younger son asked his father for his portion of his inheritance; after it was given him, he left home and wasted all his inheritance on unprofitable living. The suffering that resulted finally brought him to his senses. Note what he did.

> "But when he came to himself, he said, 'How many of my father's hired servants have bread enough and to spare, and I perish with hunger! I will arise and go to my father, and will say to him, "Father, I have sinned against heaven and before you, and I am no longer worthy to be called your son. Make me like one of your hired servants."' And he arose and came to his father. But when he was still a great way off, his father saw him and had compassion, and ran and fell on his neck and kissed him. And the son said to him, 'Father, I have sinned against heaven and in your sight, and am no longer worthy to be called your son.' But the father said to his servants, 'Bring out the best robe and put it on him, and put a ring on his hand and sandals on his feet. And bring the fatted calf here and kill it, and let us eat and be merry; for this my son was dead and is

alive again; he was lost and is found.' And they began to be merry." (Luke 15:17–24)

The young man in Jesus' conversation decided to go into the world to experience life. When he got stuck, Jesus said he came to his senses and said, "How many of my father's hired servants have bread enough and to spare, and I perish with hunger!" (Luke 15:17). He became humble.

How many of our children today are leaving home and going through tough times but cannot humble themselves to repent and return home? Many of us are going through problems but because of pride will not seek help. The pride of life sets us up for failure. Pride can even bring us to the place of saying, "I cannot eat this food or wear that thing," not because of health concerns, but because we have come to think of ourselves as better than others. If we are not mindful, we will suffer defeat in the battle of pride without even realizing we are engaged in the battle.

Let us also look at the account of the rich man whose pride cost him his life (we saw this account in chapter 1 as well, in discussing the battle of wealth). Jesus spoke this parable:

> "The ground of a certain rich man yielded plentifully. And he thought within himself, saying, 'What shall I do, since I have no room to store my crops?' So he said, 'I will do this: I will pull down my barns and build greater, and there I will store all my crops and my goods. And I will say to my soul, "Soul, you have many goods laid up for

many years; take your ease; eat, drink, and be merry.'" But God said to him, 'Fool! This night your soul will be required of you; then whose will those things be which you have provided?' So is he who lays up treasure for himself, and is not rich toward God." (Luke 12:16-21)

Wealth often encourages pride, as we see in this parable. Because of the rich man's pride, he received a guilty verdict, and the penalty was death.

We need to examine ourselves constantly and take stock of our lives, whether we are walking in pride or not. Indeed, we can walk in pride without even knowing we are doing so. This is why the psalmist prayed, "Search me, O God, and know my heart; try me, and know my anxieties; and see if there is any wicked way in me, and lead me in the way everlasting" (Psalm 139:23-24).

It sometimes takes the grace of God to reveal to us our pride. There are church leaders and leaders of this world who walk in pride and have refused to humble themselves. Because of this, their grand plans are wrecked, and they are left wondering who their enemy is when all fingers point to self. Every human being has pride. That's the way we were created by God. But we need to understand the damage pride can cause. Remember, Lucifer, the Devil, said in his heart, "I will exalt myself above God" (Isaiah 14:13).

We feel proud when we have achieved something good, whether academically, in volunteer work, or through our jobs. We are proud of our children and family members who do the right things in life. But others are proud of their acquaintances or associates, whether they do the right or the wrong things! And it is usually our associates who lead us astray in life.

So, while pride can be good or bad depending on whether our motive is good or bad, it can easily take control of us and destroy us. What is the best way to win the battle against pride? Allow us to show you a better way, which is love. With love, which is one of the five pillars of life, we are well able to win the battle against pride. The apostle Paul described love this way:

> Love suffers long and is kind; love does not envy; love does not parade itself, is not puffed up; does not behave rudely, does not seek its own, is not provoked, thinks no evil; does not rejoice in iniquity, but rejoices in the truth; bears all things, believes all things, hopes all things, endures all things. Love never fails. (1 Corinthians 13:4–8)

5.3.2 The Battle of Lust

Lust in life takes us to the extreme and causes us to become irrational and selfish, not caring or thinking about the aftermath. Lust only makes us want to satisfy our cravings at a particular time. Sometimes, in their lust for things of this world, children demand from their parents that which the parents cannot afford. But the battle of lust is fought throughout our life on the earth until the day we die. One way we can win this battle against lust is to prioritize our wants and needs. We must know what comes first in our lives, and no matter what our flesh craves, let our priority be that which is good and pleasing to God. Let us remember this battle of lust is fought in every aspect of life. It begins in our personal lives and extends into the family and outside of the home into the world. Is ordering our priorities the best way to fight and win the battle against lust? Perhaps it may be for some. On the other hand, there is a more excellent way: the five pillars of life and particularly the pillar of *contentment*.

Contentment is the only true antidote for lust. Often we get our priorities right, but we still find ourselves buying things we want but do not need. At the end of the day, you ask yourself, "Why did I buy this or get that?" And it becomes a waste. When you are contented in life, you have already won the battle against lust because contentment, along with love, peace, joy, and freedom, is one of the five pillars of life. The five pillars of life work together. When you are contented, you will have peace within, and you will not be carried away by what you see. But to reach the point of contentment in your life, you need to make the decision to get there. You should ask yourself, "Am I contented with my life?" or "Is there contentment in my life?" You have the answer to this question. We don't need to weary you any further with this issue, but we do caution you that answering the question sincerely will make your personal evaluation more fruitful.

It is imperative that you face the facts of your life and not deceive yourself. When you look into a mirror, you see yourself and no one else. You may make yourself feel good when you are among your peers and family members, but when you are alone, you know how you feel. That moment when you are alone is who you are. You are not that Hollywood celebrity who is seen by others as loving, caring, and whatever other adjectives can be used to describe your personality. Those descriptions make you feel good when you are in your Hollywood performance, and you are on top of the world. But when you get home and you are all alone, you are on the reality show, and you cannot perform for yourself. You begin to feel sorry for yourself. You find that your Hollywood appearances do not give you lasting joy or contentment. You find your life is lacking something.

We sometimes hear the shocking news that a friend, colleague, or even a family member has committed suicide when on the outside that person looked so happy and seemed to be on top of the world! Let's think for a minute. There is always a battle going on inside us that no one knows about except us. We alone have the answer to that battle. We can decide to be a winner and by the force of our willpower surrender to the *order of light,* which will bring us to a place of rest. Thus, being frank with this personal evaluation will help us wake up to the deception of the *order of darkness.*

5.3.3 The Battle of Self

The battle of self is the most difficult battle mankind faces today. Self is who we are. Self is what we are made of, our values and principles. Self consists of our dreams, our visions, our motivations, our steadfastness or persistency, our patience.

But is self the motivating force in our lives? Having the power of the third order, which is the *power to choose,* allows us to be either selfless or selfish. We need to ask ourselves every day, "Am I self-centered or selfish?" Again, we know the answer. Mankind in the garden of God fell because he took his eyes off God and placed them on self. Whenever we take our eyes off the light, we find ourselves in darkness. Self is never satisfied—never! This is why billionaires and millionaires, with all that they have, still want more! But can self be tamed? Jesus said this to His followers:

> "If anyone desires to come after Me, let him deny himself, and take up his cross, and follow Me. For whoever desires to save his life will lose it, but whoever loses his life for My sake will find it. For what profit is it to a man if he gains the whole world, and loses his own soul? Or what will a man give in exchange for his soul?" (Matthew 16:24–26)

So, can self be tamed? The answer is yes if we follow Jesus Christ. Otherwise, the answer is no. There is a reason Jesus Christ commanded His followers to deny self: The *order of darkness* appeals to our self and controls us through self. Think for a moment of the things you are doing right now. Things such as drugs, alcohol, smoking, and sexual immorality involve the satisfaction of the self. And all of these are the workings of the dark order, which we should not choose to carry out.

If those who call themselves Christians are struggling to deny themselves, we can imagine how much more self controls those who are outside of Jesus Christ! When we find ourselves centered on self, the *order of darkness* is likely going to use us as puppets. The only way not to be self-centered and self-controlled, and thus under the *order of darkness,* is to deny self. Only through Jesus Christ can we deny self by inviting Jesus Christ to come into our life and set us free from self. Remember, freedom is one of the five pillars of life. We can decide to be free from self or enjoy its misery and temporary pleasures that are manifested through the dark order. True freedom is found only in our Lord Jesus Christ, who said of Himself, "Therefore if the Son makes you free, you shall be free indeed" (John 8:36).

To begin this personal evaluation, we need to ask ourselves, "Who am I?" This question is often hard to answer. The question here is not "What have I become?" or "What have I achieved?" but rather "Who am I?" When we actually think about this repeatedly, we begin to realize that every environment, in which we have lived, whether good or bad, has impacted our lives. When I was a child growing up, I did not understand the value of going to school. Therefore, when school became boring, I saw no need to go to school except for those days when the subjects I enjoyed were being taught. Later I came to understand that education is a global phenomenon that equips and empowers people for their future careers or jobs. But as a child, I lacked knowledge of the purpose of education and thus didn't benefit from it as I should have.

In the absence of knowledge, we feel alienated from the environment. We are impacted by knowledge but often fail to benefit from it and learn from it. Because we do not know who we are, we are all over the place, trying in vain to bring the five pillars of life, or some substitute for them, into our lives. Many people believe money is the key to life, and they strive after riches—but they never seem to get enough. The fact that millionaires and billionaires are still looking for money shows that money is not the solution. Many of us have never asked who we are, so we have acquired our values and principles from what we see in the community or the society we grew up in, and that is what we have become today.

I am in the habit of asking myself questions, and this has led me to answers that have shifted my life and brought me into the fullness of this life. I can now say I'm *living* and not merely *trying to live*. Asking questions will help change our lives for the better. Not just better in the sense promoted by the politicians but better in the truest sense of allowing us to experience the five pillars of life. If people will just sit and think for a moment, they will realize they are lacking vital pillars that will bring them into the fullness of this life.

Let us go back to the beginning of mankind in the garden of God. After God's reaction to the fall of mankind, what did He say? "'Behold, the man has become like one of Us, to know good and evil. And now, lest he put out his hand and take also of the tree of life, and eat, and live forever' ... the Lord God sent him out of the garden" (Genesis 3:22–23). The fruit of the Tree of Life was what mankind needed to keep eating in order to continue living life. When God made man, man became a living soul, a being with five senses who needed the Tree of Life to live life. We share the life of this world we live in, and we know within ourselves that even though it glitters, it is not gold. We are up one minute, and the next minute we are down. This is not the life we had access to in the garden of God. If we are satisfied with the life we have but are not experiencing what true love, peace, joy, contentment, and freedom are, we are dying and not trying to live.

Who am I? I am this person who pretends to show love yet I know within myself I am filled with hatred, bitterness, and unforgiveness. Who am I? I am the one who is chasing the wind of money yet am pretending to have a lot and to have reached my goal. Who am I? I am the one who has suffered abuse from childhood, and this abuse has affected me and how I relate to people. Who am I? I am the one whose life has become dependent on drugs and alcohol because my parents were drug and alcohol addicts, and my life now manifests their abuse. Who am I? I am the one who was sexually abused by my relatives, and this has led me to become the very opposite of what a family should be. Who am I? I am the one with no confidence because of name-calling by my friends and family. Who am I? I am the one who is giving up and contemplating taking my own life because of the tragedy that has befallen me. Who am I? I am a good boy, girl, man, or woman who is a self-righteous, law-abiding citizen of the land, but the five pillars of life are lacking in my life. Who am I? I am the coward who pretends to be brave, yet I carry out my evil in the night or in deceit. Who am I?

Can you see that continually asking who you are can help you understand your true identity? The truth is, what you are today is not what God meant you to be. This is not the life you were created to live.

There are some who believe that whatever happens in our lives is God's will for us. Let us again ask the question, "Who am I?" Understanding and acknowledging the *order of light* and the *order of darkness* will help position us as people. Which of the orders operates in and over our lives? Is it the *order of darkness,* or is it the *order of light*? If the *order of darkness* is the lord and master of our lives, God has nothing to do with this. Remember, the Devil's role is to steal, kill, and destroy mankind, and that is just what he is doing. Whether or not we like it or believe it, the Devil is accomplishing his goal, and as his victims, we are helping him to fulfill his mission. On the other hand, if we are part of the light and the light reigns in and over our lives, then we are daughters or sons of God, and we live according to the spirit, as the apostle Paul described.

> Therefore, brethren, we are debtors—not to the flesh, to live according to the flesh. For if you live according to the flesh you will die; but if by the Spirit you put to death the deeds of the body, you will live. For as many as are led by the Spirit of God, these are sons of God. (Romans 8:12-14)

The question you need to ask yourself constantly is this: "Did God lead me to do what I did to others?" If God told you to do what you did, God will back you up. However, if God did not lead you to do what you did, then you are on your own. Sadly, there are people who believe they are under the light and the light is within them, but they produce the fruits of evil. Jesus said we will know them by their fruits.

> "Even so, every good tree bears good fruit, but a bad tree bears bad fruit. A good tree cannot bear bad fruit, nor can a bad tree bear good fruit. Every tree that does not bear good fruit is cut down and thrown into the fire. Therefore by their fruits you will know them." (Matthew 7:17-20)

Because of the deception of the *order of darkness,* we have lost our identity. We do not know who we are. As a result, we have been enslaved, not only to sin but also to one another. We speak of freedom and democracy, when in reality we have been bound. Because we have lost our identity, we find substitutes for our true identity, but they leave us with pain and sorrow, even while we pretend things are getting better. It is hard to pretend, though, with the levels of terror and crime we see all around us! The world is falling apart, and it—and we—will keep falling apart as long as we keep rejecting who we are. *We will die, not trying to live.* If we do not grasp the genesis of mankind's origin and identity, we will fail to find the fulfilled and abundant life characterized by righteousness and holiness, as the apostle Paul reminded us.

> And be renewed in the spirit of your mind, and that you put on the new man which was created according to God, in true righteousness and holiness. (Ephesians 4:23 – 24)

> Therefore, if anyone is in Christ, he is a new creation; old things have passed away; behold, all things have become new. (2 Corinthians 5:17)

Mankind is made in the image and likeness of God. In the absence of God, we become lost in our way for a better life. The life that is without sorrow and pain will not be experienced by all; it will be experienced only by those who are of the light. The Bible says this about those who are of the light: "God will wipe away every tear from their eyes; there shall be no more death, nor sorrow, nor crying. There shall be no more pain, for the former things have passed away" (Revelation 21:4). This scripture is speaking of a future life with Jesus Christ. However, the five pillars of life can be experienced right now if we are willing and ready to receive them into our lives.

You need to desire the light, and the light is in Jesus Christ. The apostle John wrote, "If we walk in the light as [God] is in the light, we have fellowship with one another, and the blood of Jesus Christ His Son cleanses us from all sin" (1 John 1:7). Ask Jesus Christ into your heart. Ask Him to lead you and direct you. Also, you need to renounce the dark order that has been operating in and over your life. Finally, you need to find a place of fellowship to keep your light burning, a place where the Word of God is preached, a place where sin is preached against and the believers strive toward holy and righteous living. You need to find a place where you are encouraged to read and study the Word of God and to pray. Then you can truly say, "That's who I am: one who is walking with God and living the life of God, which is eternal." And after your mortal body experiences death, you will experience this life in its true fullness.

If you find it hard to accept the light, it may not be because you are unwilling but because the *order of darkness* has full possession over you and is not allowing you to see the light. You can allow the *order of darkness* to continue being your boss, or you can do something about it. And the only thing you can do about it is to ask our Lord Jesus Christ to help you right now and to purpose in your heart to get this help from Him. Hear what He says through the prophet Jeremiah: "Call to Me, and I will answer you, and show you great and mighty things, which you do not know" (Jeremiah 33:3).

5.4   Prayer Guide for Chapter 5

God our Father and the Lord Jesus Christ has led us to write out some prayers for you to help you break through the *order of darkness* in and over your life.

The purpose of the prayer guide is to bring us into the reality of this life we are living on earth. The more sincere we are as we pray, the better the results we will experience. We present four categories of prayers designed for people at various stages of belief or unbelief. The various stages are expressed as follows: (1) I do not believe there is a God; (2) I do not believe in one God or one way to God; (3) I believe in God but have backslidden; and (4) I believe and have faith in God. As your faith grows, you can move on to the next category of prayer you believe identifies with your faith in God. It is our prayer that by reading this book, you are making progress toward believing in the almighty God, the only true God, and are moving toward the last prayer: I believe and have faith in God.

5.4.1 I Do Not Believe There Is a God

Repeat this prayer if your heart is leading you to do so.

Being sincere with You, I don't want to believe in You because I like my life the way it is. But because the prayer is a part of the book, I will pray it again.

If there is a God up there somewhere, I am speaking to You. You know I do not believe You exist or that You are God, who created the heaven and the earth and are watching over this earth I live in. If it is true that You created this world we live in and it belongs to You, I apologize for not knowing and believing in You. Even though I have heard about You from those who call themselves Christians, I have not believed this is true, and I still do not believe You are the only almighty God. If You are almighty God, let Your will be done for me to know You are God and You are out there, wherever You are. Amen.

5.4.2 I Do Not Believe in One God and One Way to God

Repeat this prayer if your heart is leading you to do so.

Again, if You are the almighty God, You know by now what is in my heart, and You know I'm not giving You the chance to reveal Yourself to me. You know all things I believe, if You are the Almighty. Again, you know I have been praying to You whose image is in my sanctified place that I have made for You. I know You are a god, and I believe in You. Nevertheless, if You are higher and greater than any god I serve, I want to know You, and I want to believe in You and in You alone. Forgive me for being ignorant when I could have heard about You. If You are the one and only God Almighty and there is none like You, through Your mercy open the eyes of my understanding and my heart to know You and to accept You as my God. As You open my heart, enable me to denounce all other gods and accept You alone as my God. Amen.

5.4.3 I Believe in God but Have Backslidden

Repeat this prayer if your heart is leading you to do so.

O, my soul says, why have I backslidden from God's free grace? Is it because God has not been fair to me? I called out to God when I needed Him, and He did not come through for me. Why is my soul still longing for You? O, God, why didn't You answer me? Where were You when I called? Where were You when my life was in checkmate? My pain, grief, and hurt remain. I see the scars and feel the shame. How can I come back to God and ask Him to come back to me? The scars have made me lose my way; the shame I feel is all that remains. Who is to blame—the One who cares for me, or me? I realize I've been deceived into blaming my God who watches over me. O, my soul, shout out and say, "I thirst for grace that quenches within, the grace that brings Christ to me, to be my Lord and save me from shame." My soul is obsessed with pain; the hurts have possessed my brain; the scars are right before my eyes; and still my soul longs to be set free. God of grace and God of mercy, pardon me today, I plead; set me free in Jesus' name, and that I may live life once again. Amen.

5.4.4 I Believe and Have Faith in God

Father God I thank You for the grace You have given me, and I do not take it for granted. I believe you are the almighty God and the Creator of the heaven and the earth. I thank You for the opportunity to discover as I read this book the truth from your Word.

Father God, I thank You for saving me from the *order of darkness* and placing me under the *order of light,* which is in and through Jesus Christ, my Lord and Savior. Lord Jesus, may You always reign in and through my life. Father God, may your grace keep me from falling into sin and keep me in Your righteousness, which comes through Jesus Christ. Thank You, God, for opening the eyes of my understanding through this book to know the orders that exist over the earth.

Father God, I thank You for showing me that not all that glitters is gold. Father God, I ask You to forgive me for walking in deception and in disobedience to your Word. Father, I pray that the spirit of deception will no longer operate in my life, and I pray that my life will experience the five pillars of life. Father, I pray that the pillars of love, peace, joy, contentment, and freedom will be experienced in my life. Father, I pray that my body will manifest good and not evil.

Father God, I believe and know life after death exists. Help me, Lord, to be prepared for this time. I know that I will have to give an account of my life here on earth. Lord, I pray that my report may be pleasing and acceptable to you. I believe and declare that my life is for Jesus Christ and is a slave for righteousness alone and will not be used for unrighteousness or for the *order of darkness.*

Father God, I thank You for allowing me to see and know who I am. Lord Jesus, I thank You for opening my eyes to the orders that exist over the earth. Father, may Your grace, which I have received through Jesus Christ, cover me and prepare me to fulfill Your will. In the name of Jesus, I pray. Amen.

Notes

Chapter 1: How It All Began

1. Oxford University Press, 2013. Oxford Dictionaries, the world's most trusted dictionaries, "Battle," http://oxforddictionaries.com/definition/english/battle (accessed January 25, 2013).
2. Farlex Inc., 2013. Free Dictionary by Farlex, "Conflict," http://www.thefreedictionary.com/conflict (accessed January 25, 2013).
3. Wikipedia Foundation Inc., 2012. "American Way," http://en.wikipedia.org/wiki/American_way (accessed December 15, 2012).
4. Socialist Alternative.org. "The end of the American dream, Class struggle on the agenda," http://www.socialistalternative.org/publications/why/ch3.html (accessed December 22, 2012).
5. Farlex Inc., 2013. Free Dictionary by Farlex, "Lust," http://www.thefreedictionary.com/lust cited (accessed January 25, 2013).

6. National Foundation for Cancer Research, 2012. "Breakthroughs in the Battle against Cancer," http://www.nfcr.org/? option=com_content&view=article&id=227&Itemid=46 (accessed December 15, 2012).

7. HowStuffWorks, Inc., 1998–2012. "Geography of Liberia," http://geography.howstuffworks.com/africa/geography-of-liberia.htm (accessed December 22, 2012).

Chapter 2: The Genesis of Reigns of Kingdoms and Nations

1. Guisepi, R., 2004. The history of the ancient Persian Empire from rise to fall. A project by History World International. http://history-world.org/persians.htm (accessed January 30, 2013).

2. Paralumun New Age Village, 2013. "History of Ancient Rome," http://www.paralumun.com/rome.htm (accessed January 30, 2013).

3. god. (n.d.). *The American Heritage® Dictionary of Idioms by Christine Ammer*. Dictionary.com: http://dictionary.reference.com/browse /god (accessed January 30, 2013).

4. MediLexicon International Ltd., 2004–2013. Medical News Today. Inside the mind of a suicide bomber, news release dated 22 June 2007. http://www.medicalnewstoday.com/releases /74879.php (accessed January 31, 2013).

5. Kumar, N. and D. Usborne, 2012. *The Independent,* Saturday 15 December 2012. America's worst school shooting: Nation rocked by massacre as gunman kills 20 children. Suspect reported to be 20-year-old son of teacher at the school. http://www.independent .co.uk /news/world/ americas/americas-worst-school-shooting-nation-rocked-by-massacre-as-gunman-kills-20-children-8417931.html (accessed February 2, 2013).

Chapter 3: Not All That Glitters Is God

1. Martin, G., 1996–2013. The Phrase Finder, "All that glitters is not gold," http://www.phrases.org.uk/meanings/28450.html (accessed January 29, 2013).

2. WiseGeek, clear answers for common questions, 2003–2013. "What is fool's gold?" http://www.wisegeek .com/what-is-fools-gold.htm#slideshow (accessed January 29, 2013).

3. Wikipedia Foundation Inc., 2013. Wikipedia the free Encyclopedia, "Wiki/United Nations Peacekeeping," http://en.wikipedia.org/wiki/United_Nations_peacekeeping (accessed February 4, 2013).

4. Yahoo UK and Ireland, 2013. Yahoo Answers, "What are the roles of NATO and how have these roles changed in recent years?" http://uk.answers.yahoo.com/question/index?qid=20060930074936AADKJBD (accessed February 4, 2013).

5. Economic Community of West African States (ECOWAS), "ECOWAS Profile.pdf," http://www.africa-union.org/root/au/recs/ECOWASProfile.pdf (accessed February 4, 2013).

6. Oxford University Press, 2013. Oxford Dictionaries, the world's most trusted dictionaries, "Love," http://oxforddictionaries.com/definition/english/love?q=love (accessed January 29, 2013).

7. Oxford University Press, 2013. Oxford Dictionaries, the world's most trusted dictionaries, "Peace," http://oxforddictionaries.com/definition/english/peace (accessed January 29, 2013).

8. Oxford University Press, 2013. Oxford Dictionaries, the world's most trusted dictionaries, "Joy," http://oxford dictionaries.com/ definition/English/joy?q=joy (accessed January 29, 2013).

9. Oxford University Press, 2013. Oxford Dictionaries, the world's most trusted dictionaries, "Contentment," http://oxforddictionaries.com/definition/English /contentment?q=contentment (accessed January 29, 2013).

10. Oxford University Press, 2013. Oxford Dictionaries, the world's most trusted dictionaries, "Freedom," http://oxforddictionaries .com /definition/english/freedom?q=freedom (accessed January 29, 2013).

11. AllAboutScience.org, 2002–2013. "The Big Bang Theory—An Overview," http://www.big-bang-theory.com/ (accessed January 29, 2013).

12. Oxford University Press, 2013. Oxford Dictionaries, the world's most trusted dictionaries, "Good," http://oxforddictionaries .com/ definition/english/good (accessed February 8, 2013).

13. evil. (n.d.). *Online Etymology Dictionary*. Dictionary.com website: http://dictionary.reference.com/browse/evil (accessed February 8, 2013).

Chapter 4: Does Life after Death Actually Exist?

1. Pravda.ru, 1999–2013. "Scientists claim life after death exists, death is only an interchange station between the two worlds" news release dated 07.11.2005 http://english.pravda.ru /society/anomal/07-11-2005/9189-soul-0/ (accessed February 8, 2013).

2. Yahoo! Inc., 2013. Yahoo! Answers, "Eternal life? What does it Mean?" http://answers.yahoo.com/question /index?Qid =20100512192930AAR4FPA (accessed January 22, 2013).

3. Got Questions Ministries, 2002–2013. "What is spiritual death?" http://www. gotquestions.orgspiritual-death.html (accessed January 22, 2013).

4. Got Questions Ministries, 2002–2013. "What is eternal death?" http://www .gotquestions.org /eternal-death.html (accessed January 23, 2013).

5. Farlex Inc., 2013. Free Dictionary by Farlex, "Survival of the fittest," http://www. thefreedictionary .com/survival+of+the+fittest (accessed January 23, 2013).

6. U4Mix-creative information website, 2013. "Globalization and New World Order," news release dated Thursday, January 27th, 2011. http://www.u4mix.com/life/globalization-world-order (accessed January 23, 2013).

7. Wikipedia Foundation Inc., 2013. Wikipedia the free Encyclopedia, "Fugitive," http://en.wikipedia.org/wiki/Fugitive (accessed January 23, 2013).

8. Montaldo, C., 2013. "Fugitives wanted by law enforcement, rewards offered for information." About.com news and issues." http://crime.about.com/od/wanted/a/fugitives.htm (accessed January 23, 2013).

9. WebFinance, Inc., 2013. BusinessDictionary.com, "Accountability," http://www.businessdictionary.com/definition/accountability.html (accessed January 23, 2013).

10. Good Governance Guide, helping local governments govern better, 2013. "What Is Good Governance?" http://www.goodgovernance.org.au/about-good-governance/what-is-good-governance/ (accessed January 23, 2013).

11. The Truth Source, helping to wake you up, 2013. "Do politicians really care about you, presidential hopefuls." http://www.thetruth source.org/opinions-rants/do-politicians-really-care-about-you (accessed February 8, 2013).

12. One World Trust, making global governance more accountable, 2008–2010. "Accountability of Global Organisations," http://oneworldtrust.org/ (accessed January 23, 2013).

13. Biblos.com, 2004–2013. *Matthew Henry's Concise Commentary on the Bible,* http://mhc.biblecommenter.com/matthew/25.htm (accessed February 12, 2013).

Chapter 5: Darkness and Light on the Earth

1. Got Questions Ministries, 2002–2013. "What is salvation? What is the Christian doctrine of salvation?" http://www.gotquestions.org/Christian-doctrine-salvation.html (accessed February 16, 2013).